PUBLISHING PITFALLS
FOR AUTHORS

MARK LESLIE LEFEBVRE

STARK
PUBLISHING SOLUTIONS

Stark Publishing Solutions

Stark Publishing Solutions
An Imprint of Stark Publishing
Waterloo, Ontario
www.starkpublishing.ca

Publisher's Note: This work is derived from the author's experience in bookselling, writing and publishing and is meant to inform and inspire writers with tools and strategies for success in their own writing path. The author and publisher believe that there is no single magic solution for everyone, and that advice, wisdom and insights should be carefully curated and adapted to suit each author's individual needs, goals and desires.

Publishing Pitfalls for Authors / Mark Leslie Lefebvre
August 2021

Print ISBN: 978-1-989351-54-3
eBook ISBN: 978-1-989351-55-0
Audio ISBN: 978-1-989351-56-7

Dedication

This one is for Randy McCharles and all of the good folks behind When Words Collide: A Festival for Readers and Writers *that happens in Calgary, Alberta every August.*

The topic and content for this book was inspired by a talk I gave at WWC *a few years ago. My experiences at this fantastic annual gathering of bookish peeps continues to inspire me in new ways every year.*

Table of Contents

INTRODUCTION:

I HAD TO P AGAIN

In September 2018, I published a short book called *The 7 Ps of Publishing Success.*

It had originally been intended as a single chapter in a much larger book I was working on. But as I kept writing it, the chapter continued to expand, and I realized I needed to explore the idea of the elements of author success in a slightly longer format.

But not too long.

It ran about 16,000 words.

Writing that runs more than 10,000 words yet less than the 40,000-to-80,000-word range of a more standard book length sits in an odd place.

It's my opinion that too many non-fiction books produced by major publishers are padded with ballast material, not to bring extra value, but so that the book "measures" properly within the market at a specifically formulated shape and size. I have found that this tendency often leads to dry repetition in many of those texts.

A book where the content could be effectively relayed in 25,000 or 30,000 words might be stretched and bloated to 50,000 or even 75,000 words.

Fortunately, early in the eBook revolution, I learned that a "book" doesn't need to be defined by such stringent viewpoints as "300 pages bound between two pieces of cloth."

A book could be whatever length serves the purpose of delivering the expected and anticipated content that satisfies the reader with what drove them to that text in the first place.

With that in mind, I decided to split that chapter on the Ps of publishing success into a book of its own. At the same time, in consultation with an editor and a business mastermind group I participate in, I decided to go with that "well-rounded" number of 7 Ps.

Those 7 Ps of Publishing Success are:

- *Practice*
- *Professionalism*
- *Patience*
- *Progression*
- *Persistence*
- *Partnership*
- *Patronage*

I even threw in an extra P for good measure, a bonus P, if you will: *Promotion*.

As I'm sure you have already intuited, the number of Ps was completely arbitrary, and a manufactured self-imposed limit was created merely for marketing purposes.

There were Ps "left on the cutting room floor" that I had written about and then either cut from the book or sneakily incorporated into the existing chapters and Ps.

Perspective was one of those Ps. *Purpose* was another one. So was *Pricing*. And *Packaging*.

One of the benefits of forcing oneself into a fixed structure like a total of seven points to cover is that it helps you create a beginning, middle, and end. An outline, if you prefer, that you can map out, plan, and then flesh out.

So, the 7 Ps, as I constructed them, seem to have done what they intended. I released the book in print, eBook, and even two different audiobook versions. One audiobook version is a self-narrated one; the other is narrated by a synthetic voice named Brian, a British male. I did that so that there could be a less expensive version available for $0.99 for those who just wanted the content in audio but didn't want the full expense. The version that I narrated sells for 5.99 USD.

Having pulled out that one chapter into its own book, I forged on, thinking I was still working on this larger book, which I was calling **Indie Publishing Insider Secrets**.

But destiny had other plans.

Another chapter I'd been working on, focusing on helping authors better understand Rakuten Kobo, took off in a similar direction. This chapter, which had so many sub-chapters and sections within it, was nearing 20,000 words when I realized that it, too, had to be split off into its own book.

The first edition of **Killing it on Kobo** was released in October 2018. That one weighed in at 38,000 words.

Back then, I had still fooled myself into believing that, now that I'd re-planted these two chapters that had grown beyond their original pots, I could go back to writing and finishing *Indie Publishing Insider Secrets*.

I naively went back to work on that book, taking a number of detours along the way, but continuing to chip at it.

A third chapter from the book, one that focused on libraries and bookstores, went the way of the previous two. However, as I continued to explore and flesh out details for that chapter, I realized that my *Indie Publishing Insider Secrets* was about to give birth to its largest baby yet.

An Author's Guide to Working with Libraries and Bookstores, released in December 2019, came in at a little over 52,000 words.

With that book out of the way, I still, rather naïvely, went back to my original book, thinking that I would have to create extremely abridged versions of the three previous texts inside that book so as not to ignore or overlook those important things I wanted writers to be aware of.

Somewhere along the way, Erin Wright, the founder of the Wide for the Win group on Facebook (a group dedicated to helping authors with publishing beyond Amazon), decided to abandon her plans to write a book of the same name.

I took up the reigns of that title (with Erin's permission and support – she wrote the foreword) and released *Wide for the Win* in March 2021.

Wide for the Win ended up incorporating much of the content I'd been drafting up for *Indie Publishing Insider Secrets*. Of course, not all of it, but enough of it that I came to think that perhaps *Wide for the Win* was replacing the originally conceived *Indie Publishing Insider Secrets*.

I still haven't decided. But one thing I have learned is the importance of adapting and evolving in my plans. (That's actually a bit of a sneak-peek into the importance of being flexible in re-adapting your **PLANNING,** which I address in this book)

But all of this is a precursor to this book.

Early in the writing of *Wide for the Win* in mid-2020, a few random concepts came to me that I wasn't able to incorporate into the book. So, I jotted them down on the whiteboard on the wall above the main writing space in my home office.

As I studied that list, I realized that several of those bullet-point items started with the letter P. I then brainstormed a whole bunch of other Ps to the mix.

Beside that list, I wrote, in a different colored dry erase marker, *7 Ps of Publishing Pitfalls*. I based that title on a one-hour talk I had originally created to give at the annual When Words Collide writer conference in Calgary several years ago. That talk was titled "Knowing the Basics and Steering Clear of the Pitfalls of Digital Publishing."

In that talk, which I have replicated numerous times, I walk through a high-level overview of digital publishing options. But I always pause to teach the audience some pitfalls and traps they can easily fall into. The pitfalls were usually in the way of the scam artists and vultures that prey on innocent authors or even clauses in digital publishing platforms to be aware of.

I wondered if I could adapt that talk into a book format.

I liked the parallel to my first book about the Ps of Publishing, and I let it sit for a while. One of the problems was that I had almost twenty items listed; so, the parallel to the sevens didn't work.

I considered doing something funky like 7 + 7 or 7 X 2 in the title. Or maybe just *14* or *21 More Ps of Publishing Success.*

Those didn't work.

I went with *7 Publishing Pitfalls for Authors to Avoid.*

When designing the cover, those words didn't flow nicely in a visual sense. It was too cluttered. So, I shortened it.

I also decided not to throw away all of the additional Ps I had collected for this book and removed the limiting 7.

The pitfalls are presented in alphabetical order and with no set or fixed length for each. Some might be a simple paragraph or two, while others take one or more pages to explore.

The idea was to outline the pitfall, explain the background or origin, where applicable, and detail elements about it, or, perhaps, symptoms for the author to recognize and, ideally, avoid. Then, I would include specific tips and strategies to help authors avoid the pitfalls.

My perspective comes from about thirty years of working within the book industry and as an author who has embraced both traditional and self-publishing (or, to use the preferred term, indie-publishing). As a result, some of the pitfalls are specifically within one side, while others apply to both indie and traditionally published authors.

In addition, just so you understand my bias and default position, I try to apply long-term thinking to each of these elements. For me, writing is a lifelong pursuit and not something that I'm involved in to try to make a quick buck. Thus, the approach that I will often recommend will, by default, take the long view.

Some of these Ps are related to the craft of writing, others to the processes, procedures, and practices, and still others to the business of writing.

Wherever possible, I have included a list of links to resources that I think would be helpful and applicable. Some may be listed at the end of a section, but most appear in a link offered under **RESOURCES** at the end of this book. If you are reading this in print or are in an environment where hyperlinks will not be effective for you to use, you can find them at the link below.

www.markleslie.ca/publishingpitfalls

My hope is that, by reading this book and being conscious of the pitfalls, you are better equipped to avoid them in your own author journey.

P IS FOR PREDATOR

Predators within the publishing industry are ruthless, heartless, and vampiric in their ways. And I'm not just talking about the blood-sucking aspect. Yes, they are proficient at sucking money from the wallets of authors. But they also have a side effect of damaging the very life-blood of hope and creativity in the authors they trick and lure. They are immortal and impossible to destroy because of the billions of dollars they collectively suck out of the pockets of writers that allow them to continue to evolve and adapt. And they have a way of mesmerizing authors, even brilliantly sharp, witty, and intelligent authors, with their powerfully convincing charms.

As mentioned in the introduction, the elements of publishing pitfalls are in alphabetical order to make it easier for writers who wanted to jump around rather than read the book cover to cover.

But it's important to spotlight, upfront, a significant pitfall that can affect all authors regardless of which publishing path they choose.

Later in this book, there is a complete chapter on predators exactly where it should fit in alphabetical order. But you need to be aware of them early on and always be on the alert. There is no garlic or holy water or wooden stake to protect you. Just knowledge that they're very real, and the only way to protect yourself is to be aware of just how stealthily they're stalking their prey.

PACE

I've broken pace into two distinct elements. The first is the pace with respect to a combination of "writing speed" and "rapid release" strategies. The second is in relation to "narrative pacing."

Writing Speed & Rapid Release

There is a lot of advice floating around within both traditional and indie publishing circles regarding pace. Specifically, that writing fast and rapidly releasing your books is the only way to find author success.

There is, of course, some truth to the fact that authors with more books in the market tend to be more likely to earn a larger income.

But for long-term success as an author, you have to remember that this is a marathon and not a sprint.

Many indie authors, particularly those who write in a series, maintain that you have to release a new book every thirty, sixty, or ninety days in order to properly ride or game the Amazon algorithms preference of new releases.

This leads some authors to write a number of books that they stockpile, then release in rapid succession over the course of a few months. For example, they might get the first three books written, edited, polished, and ready to go, then release them about thirty days apart.

One of the challenges with this type of strategy is related to reader expectation. Because, unless you can write and collaborate with your editors at that speed for a much longer term – until the end of the series, for example – you're going to be setting your readers up for disappointment.

If a reader is used to having a new novel in your series every thirty days for the first three books, then you migrate to a release every quarter, every six months, or once per year, you'll have set them up to expect one thing, then delivered another. They will be disappointed.

It is possible to leverage a rapid release schedule that is not so aggressive that you damage your mental and physical health in the process.

The key is first to determine a comfortable timeline and then pad in some buffer time – because we all know that life events can side-track or derail us most unexpectedly.

Take your time, measure your abilities and comfort level with the cycles of completing the process, and fall into the flow that works best for you.

Keep your eyes on your own lane and not on the lanes of the other writers who are releasing books faster or slower than you. Your release schedule will depend upon your actual writing pace, the process of the stringing of words together onto a page.

Unless you are just beginning your writing journey, you've likely experimented enough with your writing over time and determined a pace at which you are the right balance of comfortable, confident, and efficient.

Don't panic, worry, or stress about the pace that you write at. You write in a way that is working for you. Sure, it's okay to continue to experiment and try to push yourself, but make sure you can settle on a pace that works in the long run, a pace that allows you to breathe, pause, and enjoy the sights along the way.

Narrative Pace

While this book isn't a replacement for any of the hundreds of wonderful books about the craft of writing – nor would I dare even try to write one – the pacing or flow of the story itself that you are writing is important to attend to. And I wanted to take a moment to highlight pacing as a potential pitfall to be aware of.

Narrative pacing is the speed at which an author tells a story. A combination of factors determines the pace, such as how rapidly the action moves the story along, how quickly the narrative provides information to the reader, and the length of the scenes.

Action, description, dialogue, and narrative are elements that affect pace. Action and dialogue tend to move the story forward more quickly, while descriptions and exposition can slow the story down. An author can use sentence, paragraph, scene, and chapter length in ways that speed up or slow the story down as well.

When it comes to pacing in writing, what's most important is similar to what we explored when it comes to release timing strategy. The pacing in your story should match the expected pacing the reader expects in the genre you are writing.

Publishers, agents, and editors often reject stories and novels based on the pacing not matching their expectations. When you are indie publishing, the pacing you set can either encourage or disappoint your readers, particularly if it's not in line with what the reader has come to expect for the genre you are writing in.

Being aware of the importance of narrative pacing, and avoiding setting a pace that doesn't match your reader's expectations, is critical.

Following are a few helpful resources that you might want to look at to help you with narrative pacing.

- "7 Tools For Pacing A Novel & Keeping Your Story Moving At The Right Pace," Courtney Carpenter, April 24, 2012 (https://www.writersdigest.com/improve-my-writing/7-tools-for-pacing-a-novel-keeping-your-story-moving-at-the-right-pace)
- "Pacing in Writing: 10 Powerful Ways to Keep Readers Hooked," Reedsy Blog, October 13, 2018 (https://blog.reedsy.com/pacing-in-writing/)
- **Save the Cat! Writes a Novel:** *The Last Book on Novel Writing You'll Ever Need*, Jessica Brody, Ten Speed Press, October 2018.
- **Plot & Structure:** *Techniques and Exercises for Crafting a Plot That Grips Readers from Start to Finish*, James Scott Bell. Writers Digest Books, October 2004.
- **How to Write Best Selling Fiction**, Dean R. Koontz, Writers Digest Books, September 1981. (Out of Print as of the release of this book in August 2021)

PACK

One issue that continues to plague both self-publishing and traditional publishing circles is the "follow the pack" mentality.

Historically, traditional publishing has long chased trends and earned billions of dollars from that habit. With the popularity of novels such as Ira Levin's 1967 **Rosemary's Baby**, William Peter Blatty's 1971 novel **The Exorcist**, and Stephen King's 1974 **Carrie**, the publishing industry exploded with a deluge of horror paperbacks. Mass-produced to meet the popular demand of bloodthirsty readers (yes, the pun is completely intended), and there were more schlocky and campy-looking horror paperbacks flooding the market through the '70s and early '80s.

Publishers couldn't publish enough Young Adult fantasy novels to pick up on the popularity of J.K. Rowling's *Harry Potter* craze worldwide; sparkly yet angst-filled vampires were all the rage following the huge success of Stephanie Meyer's *Twilight* series. And there was a similar trend of erotic "poor rich man" billionaire erotic romance novels to chase the runaway success of E.L. James' **Fifty Shades of Grey**.

Publishers claim to be looking for something new, but more often than not, they are spending the majority of their publishing dollars chasing the next hottest trend.

Writers trying to chase a trend when submitting to publishers will often face a huge brick wall. Because by the time something is hot, the publishers are already moving on to something else or looking for that next hot thing.

What they want is something that's *like* the hottest latest trend, but with a new twist. And this is difficult for writers to gauge because the acquisitions teams are often looking one to two to three years into the future, rather than what is hot at the current moment.

So, if you're a writer hoping to sign with a publisher, you could fall into the trap of always chasing those trends far too late.

Indie authors similarly fall prey to those same shiny objects. First, something is hot, and an author is doing well with it. Then thousands of other authors try to mimic what they are writing and publishing, hoping to ride the wave of a massive trend.

One difference, of course, is that self-published authors benefit from publishing more quickly rather than being beholden to the red tape of the four-season selling cycle of traditional bookselling. In that way, indie authors might be able to catch a wave well before it's finished running its course.

But, when it comes to marketing tactics, this is where indie authors often miss the ball.

Speaking of balls, I'd like to use an analogy for something I've witnessed repeatedly in the indie author community since it first started to explode in 2010/2011. One or two authors do something new and remarkably innovative that allows their book or books to explode onto the bestseller lists, earning them unprecedented amounts of sales and money. That author then generously shares what they did, and the community clambers to mimic those tactics. Some of the early followers might catch enough of a benefit from being on the scene in time to pick up their own thrilling action. But the majority of other authors are madly chasing after that trend in the hopes of seeing similar success.

I equate it to the way that a group of untrained eight-year-olds might play soccer. Instead of playing their positions, they all chase madly after the one kid with the ball.

The kid with the ball heads to the far left of the field, has a blast and feels delighted that they've got the ball. Unfortunately, the rest of the pack is desperately chasing them, eager to get that ball for themselves.

Then another kid takes the ball and heads to the far right. And that giant mob all follows along to the right, eager and thirsty to have the same fun as the one with the ball.

The pack keeps shifting back and forth across the field, a mass, almost mindless, group, the majority of the players chasing and never getting the ball. Meanwhile, one or two of the kids have all the fun and "win" at this game that looks virtually nothing like the sport is supposed to.

There was a time when everyone was rushing to create a MySpace page, a Twitter account, or a Facebook profile. In mid-2021, it seems like every author is part of the stampede to figure out how TikTok can make them an overnight sensation.

And so much time, energy, and enthusiasm are spent chasing down these tactics rather than focusing on the core basics of writing or focused marketing strategies.

In most cases, if you do nothing but chase these trends after the fact, you're one of those kids chasing the kid with the ball.

Yes, there are trends within the hottest genres, and there are unique opportunities when it comes to marketing. But make sure you don't lose focus on your position within the writing and publishing sphere and that you're constantly playing to your individual strengths and following your unique path.

Trends will come and go. Things that are hot will change and morph. If you're expending energy chasing the pack, you'll always be chasing the pack. But if you play your position, you'll likely be exactly where that ball is heading at one time or another. Then, you'll be the one in control of it, instead of blinding following the pack to and fro.

PACKAGING

You can have the best book, written, edited, and polished to perfection, and ideal for your target readers to rave about. But if you don't have the right "packaging," you might fail to bring in the right readers.

In other words, your cover, and the description for your book, need to not only be professional and align with the expectations of the market, but they need to resonate with your ideal audience.

People judge books by their covers. No, it's not fair, but it is human nature. And it's something you not only need to accept but to embrace.

The majority of authors should not ever design their own covers. Yes, you might be the exception, but chances are you're not. If you do demonstrate talent in that area, you might just be falling prey to the cognitive bias of illusory superiority. This is a common human condition where a person overestimates their own qualities and abilities in relation to the abilities of other people. They default to assumptions that they are "better than average." This results in the difficulty of being able to step back and see that their cover, for example, is not as great as they perceive.

So how can you step back? Here are just a few suggestions of things to consider or do that might help you see if you are fooling yourself:

- Do you have a degree in graphic design?
- Have you ever worked for a publisher as a book cover designer, or do you have extensive experience studying the market and genre?
- Print out the cover you created and take it to a bookstore or library. Hold it up next to the other books in your genre. Does it look like it belongs? It does not need to look the same, but it should look like it belongs.
- Ask other readers – not authors, readers of your genre. Be open to their constructive criticism.

A book cover, of course, doesn't just need to look professional, but it needs to be aligned with the look and feel that is popular and understood by the ideal readers. Within the genre of romance, for example, there are distinct types of covers for different subgenres. A contemporary romance novel and a Regency romance have distinctive covers. So, too, will a paranormal romance and a romantic comedy. Or an erotic romance and a romantic suspense novel. Or inspirational romance versus steamy romance. *You* may not care about any of the differences, subtle or not, within sub-genres. But your future potential readers do care.

Your book cover needs to appeal not just to the high-level genre itself but to the readers of the sub-genre or niche.

And your books, whether they are in a series or are stand-alone books, will benefit from a common look and feel of you and your author brand. This can be challenging if you write in different genres or work with more than one publisher. But the cover should clearly indicate to the reader what that book is going to contain.

The second thing that consumers look at is the book's description – sometimes referred to as the blurb or the sales copy. Thinking of it as "sales copy" is a good idea. The job of that description is to convince the reader to click on the "buy" button when they are browsing online or to bring your book up to the checkout desk when they are browsing in a physical store or library.

If the cover's job is to capture their attention or hook their interest, the blurb's job is to set that hook firmly, so you can reel them in to "have to" read the book.

Before wasting any money on marketing, it's important to have invested the right time, resources, and money into your book's cover and description. There are plenty of services on the market available for both, and you would be well-advised to investigate and research which ones might work best for you.

Sometimes price can also be a factor in packaging, so pay attention to ensure your pricing is aligned to match reader expectations. If it's too high or too low, you'll be giving the potential reader an excuse not to make that purchase. There's more about that under **PRICING**.

PARALYSIS

It's important to gather information, learn, and break down data related to solid business decisions about your writing. Whether it's making calculations to decide which of the multitude of ideas you have that might be best to write (based on which genres are the hottest at the moment) or determining how effective different marketing strategies and tactics might be, analysis is paramount.

But be careful that you don't end up suffering from analysis paralysis.

Analysis paralysis happens when overanalyzing or overthinking a situation results in the lack of forward motion. The fear of making the wrong decision – or, more likely, not making the optimum or superior of all possible decisions – prevents any action, resulting in paralysis.

This can happen when you are trying to determine a significant plot decision or key turning-point in something you're writing, or it can happen when trying to make a business decision regarding your author journey.

While carefully planning and thoughtful decisions are necessary for a successful author career, it's beneficial to recognize when you are suffering from this ailment.

It can start with noticing what's happening. Healthy decision-making usually means outlining a range of possibilities, then narrowing down the list, crossing off items that might not be a good fit or realistically suitable. This process usually takes no more than a few days, perhaps a bit longer. So if you find yourself struggling for weeks with a list of options that **all** have equal merit, you might be in a paralysis situation with making a decision.

It might be good to consider why you are stuck in overthinking. For example, are you worried about making the "wrong" decision? Do you have difficulty trusting yourself because you previously made a similar decision, and it didn't turn out as well as you'd expected? Are you worried that others might pass judgment on you for whatever decision you make? Increasing your awareness about why you might be delaying or stalling on making a decision could provide the insights to help you overcome it.

Consider making a really small decision to "grease the wheels" of the decision-making process. Even if it's not related to writing, just making a quick small decision allows you to test your abilities and give you a little bit of confidence.

Think back to a time where you made a small, easy decision about something. It may have come with a bit of anxiety and stress, but chances are things worked out okay. Remembering that allows you to practice and grow a bit of confidence in your decision-making.

Similarly, you might want to reflect on decisions that you've made in the past that worked out well and moved things along in a positive direction. They may have even come with some hardships, but in the long run, everything worked out for "the best." Reflecting on those also reminds you that you made good decisions in the past and are likely to continue to make good decisions. In addition, it can help increase your confidence.

If you end up thinking about past decisions and ones you made that you realized, in retrospect, were mistakes (this is prone to happen because we are often hard on our past selves), don't think about the bad decision, but upon what you learned from making that mistake. Mistakes are part of the learning process, and when we make mistakes, we have opportunities to learn and grow. Try to focus on how you have grown through all of your past decisions.

And, not to belittle the importance of writing and publishing–because it is a significant part of who we are as writers–but I doubt that any writing or publishing decision we make is ever going to be life-threatening. Decisions you make might occasionally be the wrong choice or result in having to fix or re-do that work somewhere down the line, but they are rarely catastrophic. All too often, new writers can get bogged down by the sensation that the world will end if they make a mistake.

It's also important to trust your instincts and what your gut tells you. Because your "gut" often has nothing to do with logic and reasoning and more with how something feels. It can seem absurd to trust it, particularly if you prefer to rely on research and logical reasoning to make decisions. But don't forget that your personal feelings, emotions, and comfort levels with various choices and activities are definitely real and certainly unique to you. It's crucial never to lose faith in yourself and how your emotions can often help guide you to decide what feels right to you.

Finally, one of the biggest challenges is facing numerous decisions that might all feel right to different degrees. Logistically, they may all offer varying degrees of the right results. You might be stuck because you're worried about not choosing the optimal one in front of you.

Continuing to focus and dwell on the best of the best or the least bad of the bad can be exhausting and leads to more frustration and angst.

Acknowledge that you might never come to the "one right" solution. Instead, realize that you might never know what that "ultimate" answer is. Take a single minute to decide the one that feels the best, the most natural, and then accept what you've decided. Recognize that whatever it is you chose might not be perfect, and might have flaws, and might lead to other decisions or difficulties along the way.

But also recognize that you've made decisions before, you've worked through choices before, and you've made it this far. Trust yourself. And understand that this isn't the last decision you will be making. There will be more opportunities to change and adapt and learn and grow as you move forward.

If it's a decision within the content of your writing, you will always have the option to re-write or re-edit. And if it's a decision related to your author career, there are usually always new opportunities and new options that will appear on the road ahead as you continue forward.

PAST

As authors, we're often very reflective people. It's part of how we absorb information, inspiration, and insight from the people and the world around us. Then, we translate those things into the words we write and share in order to entertain, inform, and inspire readers.

But do be careful not to let the past prevent you from moving forward. Sometimes, living too much in the past can result in the **PARALYSIS** that we talked about in the previous section.

It's important to learn and grow based on acknowledging the things we have done and the decisions we have made. Whether it's something impressive and substantial that we have accomplished, or it's a mistake we made in the past, there's something to glean from it.

Sometimes we can end up spending too much time thinking about the past or speculating about the future, and not enough time focusing on the present, on the here and now, and on what we are capable of doing. Remember, we can't alter the past, and the only way we can alter the future is by what we're doing in the present.

A popular motivational quote often attributed to Albert Einstein says that we should learn from yesterday, live for today, and hope for tomorrow. He was talking about taking the lessons you've learned from the past, applying them to the things you are doing today, with optimism and hope for the future.

Oprah Winfrey is often credited with saying: "Remind yourself that this very moment is the only one you have for sure." So make the best of it.

Another pitfall related to the past that is less internally reflective is spending time bemoaning where we are in the history of writing and publishing.

There are currently five major traditional publishers out there. When I started working in the book industry, there were perhaps a dozen "big publishers." Mergers and acquisitions have cut that number by more than half in the thirty years I've been operating in this industry.

In the mid-eighties, there were twice as many major international publishers to submit a manuscript to. Publisher advances used to be extremely competitive, and it was possible (though still a bit of an outlier experience) to earn a full-time living off publisher advances and royalties. At one time, all a writer had to do was turn their manuscript in to their agent or editor and then sit back and do nothing but work on the next book and watch the royalties stream in.

Now, less than half of those major publishing options exist. Most advances are the equivalent of chump change, particularly for beginning authors. Traditionally published authors have to do more promotion and publicity for themselves than ever before.

The world of traditional publishing is different. Gone are those "golden days" of publishing.

From 2009 through 2012, you could independently publish an unedited and crudely slapped-together manuscript with a mediocre or even crappy cover. Without investing half of your time and money in paid promotions, you could still earn a significant amount of income.

That "Kindle Gold Rush" is a thing of the past.

Now, with a flooded marketplace, you have to put in a lot more time and work on polishing your book into the best it can be. In addition, you have to present it to the right demographic and likely will dedicate time and money to numerous promotion strategies.

Longing for the "good old days" and being stuck in how great the past was, whether you had the opportunity to leverage the benefits of the past or you missed out on them, is not going to move you forward.

I look at authors such as Kristine Kathryn Rusch, Dean Wesley Smith, and Kevin J. Anderson. Their careers began in the traditional publishing trenches, and they were once able to make a full-time living off of traditional publishing income.

As the industry shifted and advances dwindled, all three focused on what they could do within the shifting landscapes. They learned about indie publishing and embraced the new opportunities available to them. They adapted, grew, and strengthened the diversity of their income streams. They didn't dwell on the past; they embraced the present and created an optimistic future.

Similarly, other authors who were involved in indie publishing from the earliest days, such as Bella Andre, Barbara Freethy, Tina Folsom, and Hugh Howey, don't waste time kvetching about those "Gold Rush" days on Kindle. Instead they have focused on their readers, continued to write, adapt, and evolve as the publishing industry itself has evolved.

One thing all these authors have in common is that they have recognized that there have truly never been more options or opportunities for writers in the history of publishing.

And they are leveraging those opportunities, those options, and continuing to focus on what they can do in the present to build a continuingly successful future.

PATRIARCHY

This one is somewhat related to **PAST** because of the longstanding legacy of patriarchal power within traditional publishing. Unfortunately, the sad reality is that it's still an issue to this very day.

The business of book publishing has long been predominantly a female-driven field. Studies such as the 2019 Diversity Baseline Study conducted by independent publisher Lee & Low Books that surveyed more than 21,000 trade publishing employees, university presses, and literary agencies continue to show a higher number of female employees (74% Cis women) within publishing houses. When it comes to reading studies, women also maintain a similar dominance.

But dominance in presence does not equal dominance in pay or other displays of inequity.

When it comes to employment standards within publishing, men are paid more, promoted far more rapidly, and tend to receive higher bonuses, particularly at the senior and executive levels. A series of Bookseller articles published in March 2018 outlined a median gender pay gap at Hachette, one of the world's largest publishers, of 24.7% (with the mean/average pay gap being 29.69%). This is indicative of the numbers seen across publishing and, frustratingly, in general. Despite the book business being predominantly female, the majority of the money goes in to the pockets of men.

A post-survey article in *The Bookseller*, "Over 80% concerned about book trade gender's pay gap" (April 6, 2018), shared feelings that it truly is an Old Boys' Club type of situation:

> Meanwhile, many perceived men to be "parachuted" into senior roles from other industries and "promoted far, far faster than women" while their female counterparts struggle to rise through the ranks, which many respondents also said was less likely to happen while on, or shortly after, taking maternity leave. This was attributed partly to a "fetishisation" of men in publishing, a trade "where women tend to be more common, so men are paid comparatively more to 'tempt' them into the industry."

In addition, a Spring 2021 study by Grace E. Hanson of Portland State University, "The Patriarchy in Publishing: Examining Effects of the Covid-19 Pandemic on Women (Non-men) in the Publishing Industry," concludes that, though the Covid-19 pandemic delivered massive change in our day-to-day lives, it was especially hard on BIPOC women and non-men. Hanson states, "Closing the gender wage-gap seems impossible when the pandemic and stay-at-home-orders have set non-men back so much further than their average male counterpart."

This bit of information might only be useful to you if you are looking to work within the book industry for a publisher.

But employees at publishing companies aren't the only ones affected by this imbalance.

Historically, women have long used male pseudonyms or initials for the manuscripts and books to be taken more seriously.

The 1871 novel **Middlemarch**, broadly regarded as one of the greatest novels ever written, was written by Mary Anne Evans under the name George Eliot. Evans penned six other novels under the male pseudonym, partially because she was looking to escape the stereotype that women authors should be limited to writing light-hearted romances.

Despite their significant literary successes, the Brontë sisters, Charlotte, Anne, and Emily, published poems and novels under men's names to get reviews that weren't condescending.

After establishing herself as a hugely successful romance author, Nora Roberts released a series of futuristic mystery/police procedural novels (the ...*in Death* series) under the name J.D. Robb.

Imagine one of the richest and most successful authors in the world, J.K. Rowling, taking on a male pseudonym (Robert Galbraith) when she published her crime thriller **The Cuckoo's Calling**. Of course, prior to her being the most successful female author of this century, she adopted the more gender-neutral name J.K. Rowling to release her *Harry Potter* novels to ensure it would appeal to boy readers.

Within science fiction, an extremely male-dominated genre, authors such as CJ Cherryh (Carolyn Janice Cherry), Andre Norton (Alice Norton), and James Tiptree

Jr. (Alice B. Sheldon) adopted either male names or the gender-neutral initial option.

Prejudice and stereotypes, of course, know no bounds because there are plenty of women who release works using less gender-specific nom de plumes within the indie author space. Some of them include J.F. Penn, LJ Ross, CJ Lyons, and H.M. Ward.

At least, within the indie author community, there are more incidents where women authors represent a larger percentage of the top-earning authors. While I'm unable to reveal specifics due to confidentiality agreements, suffice it to say my years of tracking the top-selling indie authors show that women dominate the pack in this regard.

The ability to self-publish and thus bypass the gatekeepers of traditional publishing might offer more of an even playing field where the income depends on talent, persistence, dedication, and professionalism rather than gender.

In addition, the industry make-up, according to the previously mentioned study from Lee & Low Books, is 76% white, 74% cis woman, 81% straight, and 89% disabled. Fewer studies are available demonstrating what is very likely a similar discrepancy in pay, but all signs point to cis men being at the top of the income chain.

Because the patriarchy and white privilege continue to be a dominant force, writers need to be aware of where and how it might affect them when working within publishing.

PAUSE

There are two ways in which "pausing" can impact you as an author. One is the failure to pause, and the other is recovering from a pause in your writing.

First, let's look at the impact of a failure to pause.

Writers need to maintain a healthy work/life balance. As enjoyable as the act of writing can be, it's essential that we aren't working all the time. This can be challenging because, in many ways, a writer's mind never fully shuts off, even when we're not engaged in writing or typing out those words.

But pausing to ensure you are eating, resting, and relaxing in a way that aligns with what amounts to a healthy mind/body/spirit balance that works for you can be vital.

Too often, writers can get so consumed in a project that they neglect some of that balance. That can be okay short-term, particularly if it's part of an effective process that is proven to work. But it might not be sustainable in the long term and may require pausing for rest or engaging in other activities that help you maintain longevity.

A different type of pause that can be effective is taking a moment to consider your long-term goals, the tasks you are currently working on, and how they align. Perhaps other elements, either personal and internal or more external and regional and global, are having an impact. You might not be able to see such an impact until you take the time to pause, reflect, and attend to such details. Often, it's in those moments of pausing that we can take stock of things and allow ourselves a bit of a refresh and, if needed, restart.

On the flip side, one of the ways that a pause can negatively impact us is when we rely on a common pattern. You might, for example, have been in the habit of writing every morning between six and seven AM, as that's the best time of day for you where there are fewer distractions, and you're able to make solid and effective progress.

Then the holidays come around, or work, or travel, or a family issue requires you to re-align that time slot. Sometimes, pausing from the "roll" you were on, even if it's just for a day or two, can throw you off your game. And getting back into that practice can take some additional effort.

Don't beat yourself up if that happens. There will always be factors at play that take you away from a comfortable routine or process that you have built. Just remember that you never had that routine in the first place. But you managed to make it a priority and to make it happen. You developed that habit or custom through dedication, effort, and hard work. And you can, most certainly, do it again.

PAYING

This pitfall is broken down into five main areas: Paying vs. Non-paying Markets; How Free Can Pay; Payment Bleeding; Paying Too Little or Paying Too Much; Not Paying.

Paying vs. Non-Paying Markets

The concept of a "paying market" and that *money should flow to the writer* is one I maintain for all activities within traditional publishing.

When I was first working my way up through the ranks of legacy publishing, I started by sending my short stories to small press magazines. Some of them offered "payment in copy," which meant being paid with a copy of the magazine the work is published in. Then, as I slowly built up my name, I began to sell my stories for actual dollars. Sometimes a token fee might be as low as five to twenty-five dollars. And, eventually, I'd work my way up to the paying markets of between five to eight cents per word.

I cut my chops with the "payment in copy," almost equivalent to the "payment by exposure" methodology. This was, of course, in a world where the publication costs were significantly higher, and there was a crafted product to be held in one's hand.

Today, whenever a pay-via-exposure opportunity comes up, I'm extremely skeptical. I revert to the adage that *people die of exposure*. Not to mention that exposure isn't going to pay my bills. In recent years, the only time I've accepted that type of pay is when it's something I truly believe in. For example, I'm eager to support the people running the project in question, or it's a charity where I'm offering my writing in exchange for the funds being donated to a worthwhile cause.

How Free Can Pay

Free *can* pay if the author controls and leverages free as part of a larger master plan. For example, one of the most commonly successful strategies that indie authors use to earn a hearty revenue from their writing is offering their work for free, either to entice people to sign up for their author newsletter or as a way to funnel readers into their book series.

The difference here is that the author who decides to offer one or more books or stories for free is doing so with the carefully measured and calculated plan that it will lead to income (or pay) in the long run.

Having dedicated and passionate readers on your mailing list allows you, the author, to be in charge of communicating with them about new releases or timely sales of your work.

And constantly bringing new readers into an ongoing series you are writing by offering the first book for free will result in stronger sales of the remaining books in that series. That is, assuming the right readers pick it up and you've done your job satisfying them as readers.

Another way to offer your work for "free" is by making your books available through the library markets. Whether you are traditionally published (in which case your publisher automatically makes the work available to libraries) or self-published, you earn revenue whenever a library purchases your book. When you are indie published, you can leverage one or two main library sales options: OCOU (One Copy, One User) sales means that when a library purchases your eBook, they can loan it to one customer at a time forever. CPC (Cost Per Checkout) sales typically bring in one-tenth of the OCOU model, but you earn that revenue every time any patron checks your book out. It's less money up front but could result in more income in the long run.

Library reads do have a positive impact not just on discoverability but also on book sales. A 2021 Portland State University Panorama Project report showed that between 31 to 35% of people who first found a book in a library ended up purchasing that book at a brick-and-mortar or online bookstore.

Similarly, offering your books for free to advance reader teams (ARCs are Advance Reader Copies) or even to die-hard fans can lead to significant word-of-mouth marketing for you and your books.

Payment Bleeding

Suppose you engage in online advertising such as Facebook Ads, Amazon Advertising, BookBub Ads, or similar platforms. In that case, you need to be careful about how those budgets can bleed out over time.

Many authors will set up an ad and then walk away, leaving the automated systems to continue spending the budget money without ever coming back to do analytics and see if the ad results in sales. Ideally, unless your goal is to increase mailing list signups or online reviews, incoming sales revenues should be higher than the ad expenditure.

Be extremely careful here. Some of these expenditures can quickly add up, resulting in either eating away at your revenue margin or even sending you spiraling into debt. In addition, remember that if you are using a credit card to pay for an ad, your money is due within a month of that expenditure, whereas your income from the sales you generate in that same period is likely to come in forty-five to ninety days later. This creates a negative cash flow situation leading to debt that can be difficult to dig yourself out of.

Paying Too Little or Paying Too Much

You get what you pay for is a lesson that we often hear. I've been burned by this, both in purchasing less costly items that either wear out or break much more quickly than their more expensive alternatives or by hiring based on a much lower cost. I once hired an editor I could afford and got exactly the worth of the lower dollars I paid.

A good friend of mine, Julie Strauss, who is also an exceptionally talented writer and editor, has a motto she uses in this case: "Buy the best, and you'll only cry once."

Still, be careful when applying this logic. Not all of the more expensive alternatives are going to lead to the best results.

In particular, be aware of the numerous author services companies that are out there looking to charge ridiculously outrageous amounts of money selling you editing and marketing packages. Check the section on **PREDATORS** for more information about this.

Where possible, research potential professionals you hire. Regardless of the cost, check with fellow authors or author groups for personal recommendations of people and companies they have worked with and trust before dropping your hard-earned cash on something.

Not Paying

Another way that paying can become a pitfall is not paying for something and doing it yourself. Deciding not to pay for something in order to save money can sometimes be a good idea, particularly when operating on a limited budget.

But when it comes to trying to edit your writing or creating your book cover, you may end up sabotaging your writing career.

It might be possible that you can create your own book covers because you have that skill or experience. Super mega-bestselling romance author Bella Andre, who has created numerous covers for her books, is the perfect example of the exception that proves this rule. But she is the outlier here. And chances are, even if you're an excellent artist, you likely don't have the ability to craft your own book covers. Andre is a savvy businesswoman who fully understands the book market she is navigating, so her artistic talent and industry insights give her an edge that most will not have. Within the first split second that people see your book cover, they will pass judgment on it. So you need to fundamentally consider if this is an area where you want to cut corners.

Similarly, you might be the world's best editor when it comes to helping other authors with their manuscripts. But editing one's own work is extremely difficult. It might even be impossible. Yes, you may catch proofreading errors, but there's no replacement for an excellent editor who can offer developmental and copy advice to help you polish your prose. Short-changing in the editing can be as detrimental as cutting corners on your cover design.

Deciding not to pay for something can be particularly limiting once you get to a point in your writing career where your books earn you a decent income. Because once you get to that point, when fans are clamoring for more of your books, you'll often find that your time and energy are better spent on writing new material. There are numerous other tasks to offload to someone else because the cost of hiring someone for that work might be less than you can earn by spending that same time working on a new book.

PENNIES

When budgeting, strategy planning, or measuring margin, it may be easy for an author to lose track of the pennies that can really add up.

Here are just a few ways that pennies can make a difference in either a positive or negative way.

Foreign Currency Conversion

When indie publishing, authors often set their USD price and let the retail systems auto-convert based on currency exchange. This can be detrimental in two ways.

First, by not being aware of these pennies, authors can be leaving money on the table for each unit sale. And those pennies add up to dollars.

This might result in a book that is 5.99 USD being set at 7.54 CAD. At some retailers (Rakuten Kobo, for example), the volume of sales in Canada and Australia is much higher due to a larger customer base in those countries.

Based on basic consumer psychology, most people automatically round a price that they see up to the next dollar in their minds. If something costs $7.54, they need to have the rounded-up $8 to afford to buy it.

This is where the "rounded to .99" price point came from. Of course, it's only a penny below that next dollar, but since customers always round up in their minds, it seems to be a dollar cheaper.

Thus, a customer willing to spend $7.54 is not going to balk at $7.99. At the same time, they might balk at $8.00 or even $8.01 because their subconscious is already morphing that amount up into $9.

From your perspective, as an author, the difference between $7.54 and $7.99 is a mere forty-five cents. But let's say you sell an average of one copy of that book a day. That's just under $14 in a typical month. And it adds up to $164.25 in a year.

Now imagine you're leaving those pennies on the table for a half dozen books, and you're looking at $985.50. That's almost $1000 in a year of those pennies.

The other way that not paying attention to foreign currency pennies can hurt is the overall optics of your book. If the price doesn't "look right" to the local customers or merchandisers, it might give them just enough pause to move along to something else. And you never want to give either a potential reader or a merchandiser at a retailer any reason, however, small, to skip your book.

In the US, Canada, Australia, and New Zealand, the price point of .99 is universally acceptable. However, when it comes to GBP and EUR, price points of either .49 or .99 are also acceptable.

Rounding down or up to the nearest .99 or .49 in the applicable territories can make your book look more normal, like the ones published by local publishers in those countries.

And you don't want to give a potential customer *any* reason to skip your book, which can result in a lost sale. Though one or two lost sales here or there aren't much, they can add up. And if a merchandiser passes up on a title instead of including it in a featured promo, that could mean hundreds or thousands of other eyeballs not having the chance of seeing it.

Again, potential lost sales just by not paying attention to those pennies.

Bleeding Pennies

I covered this subject in **PAYING,** but it's worth expanding upon because there are several ways that you, as an author, can bleed pennies.

- **Automated Ads** – If you set daily ads in places like Facebook, Amazon Advertising, and other platforms and aren't watching the performance of those ads, the costs can outweigh the margin you are earning.
- **Subscription Services** – There are some tools and sources of information for writers that cost a monthly subscription fee. Many are beneficial and work effectively within a budget. But take care to track and monitor those services, particularly the ones you might not be using as often, to see if subscription (vs. outright purchasing, if that's an option) might be costing you a lot more in the long run.
- **Misaligned Cash Flow** – Many of the ad services that authors pay for, typically for marketing, which can grow sales, take payment via credit

cards. And, even if you measure the margin you're earning based on ad spend versus income for a month, be wary of the differentiation of the cash flow periods as well as things like credit card interest. For example, your ad costs $5.00 per day earns you $5.10 in sales per day, which means you're doing better than breaking even. You're slightly ahead. But while you owe that money *now*, you won't be receiving the earnings from those sales for forty-five to ninety days. Unless you pay that $150 a month ($5 / day) off in full, you might be paying more due to the 18 to 20% average credit card interest rates. Just be aware, and be careful.

- **Social Media** – Social media can give our brains a euphoric rush. When we interact with people or post something that gets a large number of views, likes, or comments, it stimulates that part of our author brains with the right endorphins to feel good. That can be an important and satisfying activity. But be careful about how much time you spend for that "instant gratification" rather than the more vital gratification of gaining more reviews, more sales, or more author newsletter subscribers, which you can parlay into additional revenue. Because time spent on social media is time not spent writing or engaging in business or marketing activity. And we all know that time is money.

Pinching Pennies

While it is salient to be conscious of what you are spending money on and to carefully consider your options to get the most for your hard-earned dollar, sometimes authors can be too frugal in their approach.

Spending too much time chasing down pennies might cost more than what they're worth. For example, according to *Coin News*, in 2020, it cost 1.76 cents to make a penny in the US.

In the spring of 2012, after tracking that the cost of producing a single penny cost 1.6 cents, the Canadian government stopped manufacturing them and removed them from common circulation a year later. They estimated that manufacturing pennies was costing them at least eleven million dollars per year.

Within cash transactions, this means rounding up or down to the nearest nickel. Not such a big deal. Sometimes you are a few pennies short. Other times you win out in the deal. It balances out over time. And within digital commerce, it makes no difference. But it meant that more than eleven million dollars of taxpayer money could be re-invested in other pursuits.

While the nostalgic part of me was upset with the lost penny in Canada, focusing on those pennies would be a massive waste of energy at the end of the day.

Let's say that you've had a good working relationship with a freelance editor who has to increase what they charge you. Their current rate for copy editing has been $.02 per word, which works out to about $1,600 for an

80,000-word manuscript. They have to raise their rates to $.025 per word, which moves the cost up to $2,000 for a manuscript. $400 is a lot of money, especially when you're likely earning $3.50 per unit sale. That means selling an additional 115 copies of the book to make up for that difference.

So, you spend four weeks hunting down a new editor, researching, testing numerous other editors before you find one who is willing to do that work for $0.019 per word. Sweet! That's $1520 for an 80,000-word manuscript, even cheaper than your previous editor. You saved yourself $80 off their former rate and $480 off their new rate.

But at what cost?

Perhaps you spent as many as twenty to thirty hours in your hunt for a new editor. You might have saved a few dollars, but how much is *your* time worth? That's worth considering.

Will there also be something even more important lost in the process?

The previous editor knows and inherently understands your writing and your characters. You might have built a relationship with them. They were able to work through your manuscripts very quickly because, after working together, mutual understanding and shorthand communication saved you a lot of time and energy.

It might take a significant amount of extra work and time to establish the same thing with your new editor. And it may take them longer to get into the same pattern you were used to.

Not to mention, depending on how you cut off and ended that relationship, it might have burned a bridge or given you an undesirable reputation as an author.

Just consider if all of those things are worth jeopardizing a professional relationship and potentially taking important time out of one of the most fundamental things you can do as a writer: write new material.

PEOPLE

Multiple psychological and sociological studies over the years have shown that we tend to default to the influence of the people we spend the most time with.

This suggests that the people in our lives, those we interact with, talk with, listen to, can have a significant impact and, perhaps, the largest influence on our behavior, attitudes, and results.

Harvard social psychologist Dr. David McClelland said that the people we habitually associate with can determine as much as ninety-five percent of our success or failure in life.

Attitudes and behaviors are contagious. They allow us to normalize those things into our own lives. As a result, they can have a subtle yet strong influence on who we are, how we behave, and what we do.

Are the people in your life, the ones you spend the most amount of time with, holding you back? Or are they propping you up, challenging you, and propelling you forward?

Surrounding yourself with negative people or people with habits that fundamentally oppose your ability to write and publish can be detrimental to your success as an author. But engaging with, listening to, and evolving with positive influences can help you progress.

Pay attention to those who lift you, support you, allow you to learn, and challenge you to grow in positive ways. And be aware of those whose influence works at preventing you from moving forward.

Surrounding yourself with those who lift you up rather than take you down, a sentiment commonly attributed to Oprah Winfrey, makes a lot of sense.

Authors need to be careful about who they surround themselves with because it's not always easy to detect who is lifting you up and who is trying to put you down.

But both the people in your life who believe in and support you and your dreams and the author communities you engage with can have a subtle yet powerful impact on you.

There are, even within the indie author community, hundreds, perhaps thousands of isolated silos of communities, echo-chambers of the same advice, where the members who aren't interacting beyond those silos can't even see the possibilities that exist outside the attitudes, beliefs, and habits of the majority of that group.

From time to time, it's important to pause and take a look around. Who and what is having that subconscious effect on your author life and potentially holding you back from your full potential? Similarly, on the positive side, who is propping you up, pushing you forward, challenging you to learn, grow, and become a better writer?

PERCEIVED BORDERS

This chapter is associated with traditional publishing and is a pitfall related to how perception can prevent or limit opportunity. However, when you are aware of the imagined or perceived borders within traditional publishing for digital products like eBooks, it opens up opportunities for you, both within self-publishing and traditional publishing.

Historically, publishing has been about acquiring the rights to works for distribution and sale within specific territories. Publishers in the United States, for example, would buy US rights. Publishers in Canada would buy Canadian rights. Publishers in the UK would buy UK rights. And so on and so on.

They have "on the ground" editorial, marketing, and sales teams to work with the local bookstore buyers. They also either have their own distribution warehouses or leverage a domestic warehouse to ship their books into the market.

It made no financial sense to purchase the rights to a book for a territory you couldn't sell it in. So, an editor at one publishing house in the US would buy the US rights to a manuscript, while a different publisher would buy the UK rights, for example.

Indie authors, you have to remember I'm talking not just about pre-eBook days (the Kindle launched in 2007, but E Ink readers were around since the late 1999s), but pre-internet.

As publishers grew and became more international, there would sometimes be collaborative rights purchased across territories. An editor at Random House Canada, for example, would be interested in purchasing a manuscript that they believed would also work for their colleagues in the US and the UK. They would then potentially purchase multiple territories at a reduced rate in a "buy more, save more" manner.

Agents would work to earn the most for an author's manuscript by playing publishers off one another, particularly if more than one acquisitions editor at different publishing houses were interested in it. They would hold out for a much larger advance for selling rights to two or more markets because they might earn more by splitting the rights. For example, they could earn a US $50,000 advance for each of the US, CA, and UK rights (a total of $150,000), instead of selling the rights in all three territories to a single publisher for $100,000.

This is how the traditional publishing world operates. It's why major book fairs would take place annually in Germany, the UK, Paris, New York, and Canada. These events were about acquiring international/foreign works and intriguing bookstore buyers about already acquired and forthcoming titles.

When eBooks came around and, in particular, self-publishing, there were no more borders. eBooks didn't need to be put on a boat and shipped overseas and stored in a local warehouse. Instead, servers had a global reach.

So when it comes to publishing a book on Amazon via Kindle Direct Publishing, or using Kobo's direct publishing tool Kobo Writing Life, or a distribution platform like Smashwords or Draft2Digital, worldwide rights were assumed. If the author hadn't sold the work to a publisher, they still had all the rights and could allow the book to be released globally and available for sale in numerous countries simultaneously.

(I'm simplifying this because Amazon doesn't actually reach all countries in the world. But Kobo does. And Smashwords. And Apple Books.)

By default, indie authors are hardly aware of the perceived digital borders, traditional publishers mostly still operate under that principle. That's because most of their business model (and a significant portion of their revenue) is tied directly to local warehousing and shipping of physical books through the book market. Since the global Covid-19 pandemic, some of the savvier publishers have started to open their eyes and minds to the global nature of eBooks and digital audiobooks. However, they are still operating in a significantly different mindset than indie authors. This is one of the reasons why the two groups don't often see eye-to-eye about strategies.

As an author, being aware of this could allow you to earn even more money than you are by blindly charging forth and either selling numerous country rights in all formats to a publisher or, on the flip side, self-publishing.

So, if you have signed a contract with a publisher for a book, check to see which territories they have purchased rights for. They will often purchase all format rights in specific territories. If, for example, they only acquired the US and Canadian rights, you can still license/exploit the rights in other territories. You, or your agent, can license those other rights to other publishers. Or, you can use the self-publishing platforms like Kindle Direct Publishing, Kobo Writing Life, and Draft2Digital to publish the eBook in **only** those unserved territories.

A relatively recent example of this was when Canadian Science Fiction author Robert J. Sawyer released the novel *The Oppenheimer Alternative* in 2020. He split the rights for the print edition to two different publishers. One is a Canadian publisher (Fitzhenry & Whiteside Limited), and the other a US Publisher (Arc Manor's Caezik SF & Fantasy imprint).

Rob is a big enough "name" author that he was able to negotiate maintaining global eBook and audiobook rights. Indie authors have long been more adept at proficiency and effective strategy for eBook sales than most traditional publishers. With his previous novel, *Quantum Night*, he sold print, eBook, and audiobook rights to Penguin Random House in Canada and the US, while maintaining the rest of the global rights. He found that he sold far more eBooks outside of CA and the US than PRH was able to sell in North America. They priced their version at about $14.99, and he priced his version (only available outside the US and CA) at $4.99. Not only did he outsell the world's largest publisher in terms of units of the self-published eBook, but he earned 70% of the $4.99 sales, getting paid monthly. In comparison, while the traditionally published eBook earned him closer to 10%, paid out only bi-annually.

Sawyer then licensed audiobook rights to Recorded Books.

His awareness of the perceived borders in traditional publishing allowed him to maximize his reach into different audiences per format and the margin he earned on those sales.

You can learn more about Rob's strategies and publishing history via two different interviews I did with him for the *Stark Reflections on Writing and Publishing* podcast. He appeared in Episode 004 – Optimizing Your Author Brand with Robert J. Sawyer (January 26, 2018) and Episode 145 – Leveraging your IP and Hybrid Publishing with Robert J. Sawyer (July 31, 2020).

And, as you move forward, be aware of those perceived borders in a connected digital world and how you might be able to split rights in dynamic ways to help increase your earning potential.

PERCEPTION

The limits of our perception are always difficult for us to see. We are products of the environment we grew up in, the influences on our lives, and the experiences we have had.

It's extremely hard to see beyond the limits of our perception. Thus, it is also tough to see where that perception is limiting our opportunities as writers.

For example, I'm fortunate to have worked within the book industry for numerous decades. It has allowed me to see, experience, and understand both traditional publishing and the indie publishing communities.

I understand some of the behaviors of the large publishers and traditionally published authors that indie authors shake their heads at in bewilderment. But, on the flip side, those on the traditional side of the industry (both publishers and authors) often still believe that those who self-publish are doing it because they're not good enough to be represented by a "real" publisher. They also believe that if it's not released through those legacy means, it hasn't been edited and is likely not well-written to begin with.

Indie authors often fail to see that traditional publishing is operating and approaching bookselling in a print, warehouse, and distribute model that is still a significant percentage of their revenue. As a result, they can't understand why most publishers aren't able to adeptly operate and embrace eBooks or why they price their eBooks higher than the typical mass market paperback price levels. There are inherent fears within publishing that eBook sales will cannibalize those print sales which still account for upwards of 80% of their profit margin. Their entire ecosystems, company structures, and processes were built on and still thrive upon selling physical books and the "windowing" of releases from the more expensive to the lesser expensive formats for books.

Let me share a simplified example of how the book industry "windows" the release of formats.

A book released in hardcover usually remains in hardcover for nine to twelve months, typically so that it can exist in that most expensive format for the Christmas season, the most significant selling season in the book industry. (Historically, many bookstores would operate in the red for two or three seasons and make the majority of their profit in the fourth quarter of the Christmas season, more than making up for their losses the rest of the year).

After that book has done its tour of duty through Christmas in hardcover, the paperback would be released. Typically, a trade paperback uses the same "printing plates" as a hardcover edition (so there are cost savings). The price is lower than the hardcover but still more expensive than a mass market edition. Again, it runs about a year; if the publisher does produce them, a mass market (pocketbook-sized) edition comes out at the lower price.

When eBooks came along, they threw a monkey wrench into that "windowing" process. Publishers originally wanted to release the eBook after the mass market paperback to not lose money off sales of the more expensive versions. That's one of the reasons why they settled on prices that are more in line with the trade paperback editions or, sometimes, even higher.

It's partially trying to adapt their existing model into a new format that transcends that model.

Because indie authors make most of their income off of eBook sales, and most often, their print book sales are even smaller than the traditional publisher's share of eBook sales, indies think that traditional publishers are insane to be over-pricing their eBooks and missing out on fantastic revenue opportunities.

As our world becomes more and more divisive, with pockets and silos of people rallying in their own groups and not listening to what the others have to say, that divide gets larger. We end up relying on the very powerful confirmation bias that drives us, mostly subconsciously, to seek out and only attend to information that supports our pre-existing beliefs. It also results in our decrying the evils and insanity of "the other." And it becomes far more challenging even to realize that we are limiting ourselves.

In order to break out of a limited perception, here are some things you might try.

Look for ways that you can challenge what you think you are seeing. For example, discuss your thoughts on the matter with others. And try to discuss it with a diverse group of people, not just the "yes men" who confirm your perspective. A proper "devil's advocate" can be helpful to help chew on alternative ideas and perspectives.

Try to recognize if you are relying on anchoring bias. This is where you jump to conclusions or base your final decision on that original, or first, perception you had about something, rather than absorbing the newly acquired facts or perceptions that might challenge or upset that initial view. Forcing yourself to decide more slowly, rather than rushing to a conclusion, can be one way of ensuring you're not limiting yourself with that anchored belief or perception.

You may even pause to consider something using psychologist Edward de Bono's *Six Thinking Hats* methodology. The premise behind it is that the human brain has distinct ways it thinks and processes information. One can perceive it from numerous viewpoints by consciously approaching a challenge by "switching hats" or temporarily wearing a different type of thinking cap.

The hats are:

- **BLUE** – Process – Thinking about Thinking. Planning. Organizing. Considering what thinking is needed.
- **WHITE** – Facts – Collecting Data. Asking what is known? What is needed to know? How to obtain that information?
- **RED** – Feelings – Intuition, hunches, gut instincts. Understanding what is felt right now. No reasoning involved.
- **GREEN** – Creativity – Openly considering ideas as they flow. Alternatives and possibilities.
- **YELLOW** – Benefits – Focusing on the positives, the pluses, the gains. All aligned with logic.
- **BLACK** – Cautious – Recognizing the difficulties, the challenges, the risks, and the dangers. Also aligned with logic.

PERFECTION

Don't let perfection be the enemy that prevents you from completing a book.

This is challenging because authors need to ensure their work is the best it can be before submitting it to an agent or editor when taking the traditional publishing route or, if they are an indie author, before releasing it into the market.

However, authors also need to be cautious that the desire to "take one more pass" at re-writing or re-editing a manuscript may be a stalling tactic. It might be slightly hidden procrastination preventing them from taking that risk of publishing.

Yes, your book needs to be excellent. It needs to be edited, proofread, polished, and aligned to your target market in as many ways as possible.

But it will **never** be perfect.

I've worked in the book industry since 1992, and I can assure you that if you walk into virtually any bookstore or library and pick up almost any book on the shelves, you are bound to find at least a handful of typos. It doesn't matter if it's a book from an indie author or a title from the world's largest publisher. They happen. And catching all of them is almost as frustrating a task as shoveling water.

I can also look at books of my own (again, either the ones I published myself or titles published via a traditional publisher) and still find typos, errors, and things I would like to change or tweak if I wrote it today.

But if I were to spend all my time focusing on that instead of writing new material, where would I be?

Likely an author with a grand vision or dream to publish my first book.

For many authors, getting that first novel out is a major hurdle and a milestone accomplishment. It might have taken years, or even decades, to work up to that point. And often, once an author gets that freshman or sophomore "year" behind them, they can put that stalling behind them.

When an author recognizes that it'll never be truly perfect, they can move forward.

In his moral poem *La Béguele,* Voltaire quoted an Italian proverb when he wrote, "*…le mieux est le ennemi du bien.*" This line is often translated as "perfect is the enemy of good."

This led to the more modern adage: **Perfect is the enemy of done**.

Don't forget that, in your desire to polish, re-write, research, and prepare. Make sure that you're making forward progress and not just stalling.

As Seth Godin has expressed, the only purpose of starting something is to finish it. And, while the projects we do may never really be finished, they must ship. Because, as Godin concludes, if it doesn't ship, it doesn't count.

PERMANENCE

There are two ways that permanence can harm you and your writing career.

The first is what you say, share, and post online.

The second is related to contracts terms and deals you sign.

Online

I was lucky to have grown up in a world where the digital recording of behavior wasn't common, nor was I able to post something to online social media that could come back to haunt me.

Sure, I made plenty of mistakes. In my very first appearance at an in-person convention in the early 90s, when I'd done a reading a Q&A session on writing horror, I was cocky and smarmy and had only sold a handful of short stories to some small press magazines. And yet, I had the gall to publicly criticize the artist who illustrated one of my stories. I'm still embarrassed by that behavior and am fortunate that this wasn't something a person could pick up their phone, record, and post all over the internet.

I'm lucky, I suppose, that this event isn't something that could be splashed all over the internet. I realized that it was wrong after I'd done it. I learned. And I grew and changed my behavior.

But not everyone is that lucky. Especially not today.

Consider, in recent history, *any* writer, actor, musician, or politician that you've seen getting caught doing something very wrong. It happens all the time, and it doesn't seem to matter what amazing things they have created or any of the good they have done – they are judged by that one blatant act of assholery.

Things you write, share, and post will come back to haunt you. I'm not saying to avoid social media or creating and sharing content in the online world. That's practically inevitable. But I am suggestion you proceed with caution. And that you take care. Take a moment to consider those things you might be tempted to respond to or post in the heat of a moment.

Contracts

Writers need to be far more careful when signing up to contract terms, both within traditional publishing and self-publishing.

It used to be that rights reverted back to authors on a traditional publishing deal after a book is out of print. But what does the term "out of print" mean today in the realm of print-on-demand (POD)? And with more and more smaller publishers using POD technology rather than the more traditional offset printing and warehousing, it might mean books never go out of print.

A common publishing contract clause involves signing over the rights for future technologies that might not yet exist. It sometimes uses language such as "all media now known or hereafter conceived or created." Signing or agreeing to such a term locks you in and can mean the loss of significant revenue. Moreover, it means you're handing over those rights without even knowing what they are or how you might leverage them if you were to maintain control of them.

One of my pet peeves is that most authors sign contracts for direct/self-publishing without actually reading or understanding the contracts they are signing up for. This is for the rights/licensing of their hard work, those precious "babies" they spend so much time carefully crafting and nurturing.

Or, they might agree to an option within a contract where they hand over exclusivity to one retailer. Kindle Direct Publishing's ninety days of exclusivity is relatively small. It's only three months, which isn't a big deal. But thousands of authors learned the hard way that agreeing to seven years of exclusivity on their audiobook rights with ACX (Amazon's Audio Creation Exchange) felt like a century. The short-term gains - a slightly higher margin and not having to pay narrator fees upfront, simply weren't worth it.

A **lot** can change in seven years. Just go back seven years from today and look at significant changes in the world. Personally, my life is significantly different than it was seven years ago. But in a world-view, think about the incredibly divisive and hostile world of politics related to Brexit in the UK or the reign of a former reality show businessman grifter as President of the US. And that's not to mention the impact of a global pandemic that dramatically charged onto the scene in early 2020.

Like I said, plenty of things can change in seven years or less. Having your rights locked up can feel, in those years, like a permanent prison.

There's a bit more about contracts and clauses to be careful about under **PUBLISHERS**.

PERSPECTIVE

As writers, we need to constantly be learning, listening, watching, absorbing, and growing.

But it's so important that while we are learning, we also take things we hear, read, or learn about with a grain of salt.

Every source of information comes with a particular view, bias, or even preconceived notion. You'll likely have noticed my personal biases by the time you got to this part of the book. That's because, while I believe I've done my best to try to share things I feel will benefit authors, I've approached this topic of publishing pitfalls with hundreds of my biased viewpoints.

I likely have already put off some readers who either took offense to something I criticized or disagreed with me so vehemently that they stopped reading, threw the book down in disgust, and maybe even went on to leave a one-star review.

Sometimes, as writers, we hear about something, or a well-intended author or industry person shares something that they are genuinely and honestly trying to help other authors with.

But I caution you that even if the person is well-intentioned, they are sharing their knowledge, insights, wisdom based on biases and perspectives that are uniquely theirs.

For example, I like to believe my intention in writing this book is to help authors avoid various pitfalls within writing and publishing. My own experience includes licensing rights to traditional publishers as well as self-publishing. So I'm open to both. I also worked as a bricks-and-mortar bookseller for years, so that skews my perspective. Having worked at Kobo for six years and working with Draft2Digital since late 2018, I bring a bias toward publishing "wide" well beyond Amazon's KDP exclusivity terms. I'm also a cisgender, heterosexual, middle-aged, tall (6'3"), white male. My perspective comes from a place of definite privilege, both in the real world and within the world of publishing. So, I am likely not even aware of other challenges other writers might face and didn't raise them as a pitfall.

You, too, bring your own unique and powerful perspective to everything you experience and learn.

Take care to be aware of your perspective and the perspectives of those you interact with.

Blindly accepting something as truth or "the only way" can limit you in significant ways in your author journey.

For tips on dealing with this, refresh yourself with the ideas offered under the chapter on **PERCEPTION**.

PILE UP

Whether you are writing full-time or writing while working a full-time job, there will come times when the work, emails, paperwork, and other tasks pile up in front of you.

One of the challenges when things are stacked so high (whether it's virtual or physically in front of you) is that they can cause you stress. Sometimes, you aren't even consciously aware of the stress, but it's there, and it makes working more frustrating.

For example, I'm writing this in the morning before moving on and doing other tasks. But occasionally, instead of focusing on this writing, my mind wanders back to my email inbox. And I'm bothered by the more than fifty new emails that came into my inbox overnight, as well as the additional ten I had flagged to follow up with today after I finished my writing.

To the right on the desk I'm sitting at is a contract from a publisher, numerous check stubs, paid bills that I have to file, and a small stack of paperbacks I'd pulled for researching a novel that I have yet to re-shelve. They're visible, and I'm consciously aware of those "to do" tasks, distracting me from effective and focused writing.

At my standing desk on my left is a print-out of a conference schedule that I have to create presentations for, more paperbacks I had pulled out to demonstrate as examples in a live virtual book event I was leading, and a

DVD and book that are future research for another forth-coming book project that I've barely started.

All this is to say that, without turning my head from the screen I'm looking at as I type these words, I can see several unfinished tasks in my peripheral vision. I'd like to believe that they're not causing me stress, but I am aware of how they may impact, and even slow, my progress.

An unclean or untidy work environment can negatively impact your productivity and effectiveness. It could be as much as how you can't sit down to work without first shifting a giant pile of papers and other materials from your desk and chair. Or it might be a small, distracting pile. On the other hand, an empty or well-organized work space might mean being able to jump directly into writing.

An overflowing inbox or other tasks on your writer plate might also be causing you stress. And that's why prioritizing and saying no to some tasks, requests, or asks can be healthy. Saying yes to everything, then over-whelming yourself with an endless "to do" list can be detrimental to your mental and emotional well-being, negatively affecting your writing.

One way to deal with pile-up is to invest the time into organizing your workspace and the way you file. There's no one way to do this, just the way that works best for you.

Another way is taking the time to prioritize those things that are "piled-up" on your to-do list. That's discussed a bit more under **PRIORITIES**.

PINOCCHIO

I'm not using Pinocchio, the name associated with the fictional character created by Carlo Collodi of Italy in 1883, in the way you might imagine.

When most people think about Pinocchio, they remember his tendency to tell lies and that his nose grows whenever he speaks a mistruth or is deceptive. However, that's not what this chapter is about.

The wooden puppet created by Geppetto, the woodcarver, can walk, talk, and interact on his own. But he dreams of becoming a **real** boy. A fairy tells Pinocchio to prove himself brave, truthful, and unselfish, and someday he will be a real boy.

Unfortunately, no matter how many brave, truthful, and unselfish accomplishments a writer experiences, they may never feel like a "real writer." This is known as *imposter syndrome,* and it is a real and common affliction that writers experience.

Imposter syndrome refers to the internal experience of believing that you are not as competent as others perceive you to be. It can come from a tendency to downplay, discount, or diminish obvious evidence of our abilities.

Even those writers who have achieved unprecedented awards, accolades, and international bestselling status that most writers can only dream of suffer from it.

Poet, memoirist, and civil rights activist Maya Angelou, who received dozens of awards and more than fifty honorary degrees for her work, was quoted as saying, "I have written eleven books, but each time I think, 'Uh oh, they're going to find out now. I've run a game on everybody, and they're going to find me out.'"

Joanna Penn, podcaster (*The Creative Penn*) and author of **The Successful Author Mindset**, once shared an experience at ThrillerFest in New York. At a panel discussion were R.L. Stine, Lee Child, Sandra Brown, David Morrell, and Clive Cussler, authors who have collectively sold over 600 million books and been translated into at least thirty-five languages. All of these notable authors admitted that they still feel that way.

"All this means," Joanna says, "is that self-doubt is part of the creative process." She also says: "In fact, if you don't feel any kind of doubt, there's probably something wrong."

Poet Charles Bukowski once lamented in an interview that "Bad writers tend to have the self-confidence, while the good ones tend to have self-doubt."

Doctor Valerie Young, an internationally known speaker, author, and leading expert on impostor syndrome, says that talking about imposter syndrome is a start, but you can't share your way out of it.

Here are ten tips, adapted from Dr. Young's suggestions, of ways to stop thinking like an imposter:

1) **Break the silence** – acknowledging and admitting to these feelings, or "fessing up," is a good start. Admitting this to other writers might help. But admitting it to yourself first is important, too.

2) **Separate feelings from fact** – recognize that there will be times you feel stupid and that it happens to everyone (or at least, everyone smart enough to realize they don't know everything.) Good writers become great writers when they realize they don't know everything and try to learn something new every day. And that learning is what makes them better, not something that makes them dumb or imposters.

3) **Recognize when you should feel fraudulent** – there may be times when you lack a sense of belonging because of your differences from the rest of the "pack" in a situation. Be sure to acknowledge that so it doesn't get the better of you.

4) **Accentuate the positive** – a good thing about being so hard on yourself is that it's likely because you care about the quality of your writing. That's a great thing. You care. Your writing is better for it.

5) **Develop a healthy response to failure and mistakes** – instead of beating yourself up, recognize that failure in something is an opportunity to have another go at it by learning from a mistake you made. A sentence, scene, character, plot twist, or whatever can be adjusted if it's wrong. But you can't edit something that isn't written.

6) **Right the rules** – you have just as much right as any other person to be wrong, make mistakes, take a break, or ask for help when you need it. The

writing community is tremendously supportive. Reach out and ask if you don't know. You might be surprised at how willing fellow writers are to help you.

7) **Develop a new script** – Be conscious and aware of the self-doubt talk you're hitting yourself with. Instead of worrying about people recognizing you "have no idea what you're doing," acknowledge that you're learning as you go. Or, if you find yourself amongst peers you regard as successful or brilliant, consider how fortunate you are to be able to learn from and interact with them. I've been lucky enough to share the stage with Margaret Atwood, Alice Munro, Michael Connelly, Joanna Penn, Peter James, Hugh Howey, Kristine Kathryn Rusch, Dean Wesley Smith, and dozens of other internationally bestselling authors. It didn't happen by accident. I worked hard, and that's how I found myself there. You're also likely among others in your field that you admire, respect, and look up to because you're being recognized as having similar traits and skills.

8) **Visualize success** – instead of imaging doom and failure, do what athletes do and spend some time imagining the success of the sales of your new book. Or, imagine a talk, reading, or interview where you nail it.

9) **Reward yourself** – External validation is good, but it's also important to be able to pat yourself on the back for the hard work you put into something.

You finished the first draft? Great! Acknowledge that success. Most people will never do that.

10) **Fake it 'til you make it** – recognize that sometimes all of us are flying by the seat of our pants, sticking our necks out, and hoping for the best along the way. Waiting until the confidence happens might never occur. But taking a chance and "acting" confident might be enough to get you into the right frame of mind to be confident.

One last thing I'd like to share about confidence, self-doubt, and imposter syndrome stems from a fantastic "Eggs Benedict" talk that my good friend James A. Owen often shares at Superstars Writing Seminars. Ultimately, both downplaying your accomplishments and exuding confidence in what you've achieved can dramatically affect on the way others perceive you.

In his book **Drawing out the Dragons**, James writes, "no one ever inspired anyone else to greatness by pretending to be less awesome than they really are."

Let's face it. If you've written a book, you're already pretty darned awesome. Most people say they want to write a book. But most of them won't. And you've already accomplished that.

So don't dream of being "a real author" one day. You already **are** a real author today.

PLANNING

There is no one way to plan. The right way to plan is the way that works best for you and your goals. But you do need to have some sort of blueprint, no matter how you conceive, capture, and track it.

The reality is that, as Antoine de Saint-Exupéry said, "a goal without a plan is just a wish."

And whether you plan and plot out your novel with a detailed outline or you prefer to "pants" or "discovery write" your way through a manuscript, you're likely going to have to scope things out along the way. First, you'll need to determine when and how you're going to get it written. Then, you have to map out the publishing path that you believe will work best for that book, i.e., what agents or editors to submit it to, or which ways and tools you'll use to publish it yourself.

Neglecting to plan your overall goals as a writer and the way you'll start and finish a book or how you move into publishing can be ultimately detrimental.

But not being flexible with existing outlines can also hold you back and prevent you from finding success.

There is an old Yiddish proverb that says: "Man plans, God laughs." This is because not everything goes according to the intended scheme. Life can be unpredictable, and unexpected and unplanned things can happen along the way.

All of those things that occur as you are in the middle of making progress can make your plan seem out of date or useless.

But here's the brilliance of scoping things out ahead of time.

The original blueprint that you created isn't carved in stone. It's malleable, flexible, and adaptable.

When the unexpected seeks to throw you for a loop, pause to consider how you might be able to readjust and realign your plan.

I'll offer a few examples. Several years ago, my original plan to get the first draft of a manuscript done was to get up an hour earlier than I had to get ready for a work commute into Toronto from my home about a one-hour drive away. That worked wonderfully until a combination of construction and increased traffic congestion meant I had to start leaving for work earlier and earlier to get in on time.

It wasn't feasible for me to keep pushing my wake-up time earlier and earlier, and, after about a year and a half, that hour became forty-five minutes, then half an hour, then fifteen minutes, then it was gone.

My plan to write before work in the morning was no longer possible – not without losing more sleep. So, I re-adjusted my schedule to find other times and days to get those same number of hours I'd lost (five in total for the week). And I re-planned accordingly. I found about half an hour every day at lunch, which came to two and a half hours. Which meant I only needed to carve out another two and a half hours elsewhere in my week.

Taking a step back, absorbing new insights, new situations, changes to the environment that affects your original plan, and then re-scoping can help. It's one of the ways that you, as an author, can "laugh back" in the face of the adversity that is evitable, instead of throwing up your hands and crying in frustration.

POUNCING

Trends come and go within the publishing industry, within genres that are "hot" and "on the rise," as well as within marketing tactics and social media platforms.

It is always tempting to pounce on that next great thing, jump on the bandwagon, or get caught up in the latest trend sweeping the author community.

While it's important to be constantly learning, growing, and engaging in new opportunities, platforms, and interactions, be sure that you're not behaving in that "shiny object" behavior of pouncing on some cool new thing to the detriment of your long-term plans and goals as an author.

Experimentation and trying new things are critical as you continue to learn and grow, but take care not to be overly consumed with jumping on a trend for the sake of jumping into it, particularly when there's a lot of buzz on how this shiny new thing is *the* magic bullet that will the help your sales skyrocket.

It's critical to step back, analyze this new trend or activity, and see where and how it aligns with your long-term goals and plans for your author career. Sometimes it might require spending some time testing the waters or engaging in whatever it is before you can get a solid feel for it.

But be careful that the new thing you pounced on isn't consuming more time than it is worth and that it does align with your abiding goals.

PRACTICE

In my book **The 7 Ps of Publishing Success**, I ranked **PRACTICE** first. Within both the craft of writing and engaging in the business of writing, practice is critically important for a writer.

The more you write, the better you become at it.

But be aware that there is a caveat to this.

Practicing in the wrong way or the wrong habits can be detrimental to your growth as a writer.

Performing the same task over and over in the wrong manner, without learning, growing, or adapting new knowledge, insights, or techniques, is merely going to stifle you as an author.

It's going to lead you to poor habits that negatively impact your ability to grow and prosper.

If, for example, you have a tendency to make the same mistakes in grammar or within the plots or character developments, and you don't learn from them, you might be practicing a bad habit.

Take care to ensure that you're not practicing the wrong things and ingraining habits that are detrimental to your learning and growth related to the craft of writing.

The same is true for the things you do when it comes to the business of writing. Whether it's in submitting your work to traditional markets, or the processes you use for indie publishing, there might be practices you do because you have "always done it that way" that are limiting your growth.

Practicing and becoming better at something only works when you can see and understand how the practice is improving your skills and abilities. If you reach a plateau of growth, you might end up stuck in a rut that's difficult to grow out of.

That is why, as I further discuss in the aforementioned *The 7 Ps of Publishing Success*, **PRACTICE** without **PROGRESSION** can be something that holds you back as a writer instead of moving you forward.

PREDATORS

Predators are one of the most significant pitfalls facing authors. Yes, I know I teased it out at the very start of this book because, alphabetically, it comes along much later, but I was also tempted to present this chapter in **bold ALL CAPS** text using at least an 18-point font.

It may seem dramatic, and I wish I didn't have to be dramatic about it. But that's just how dangerous and prevalent book industry predators are.

Predators are working within almost every aspect of writing and publishing. Regardless of whether you choose traditional publishing or self-publishing, the water is rife with them.

Over the years, they've existed under different terms. Vanity Publishers is an often-used term that has appeared as early as 1941. Here is an excerpt from a 1958 *Library Trends* article by Howard A. Sullivan called "Vanity Press Publishing."

Subsidy publishing has risen to its present statistical eminence from the debacle brought about in 1941 by the federal government's conviction for mail fraud of C. Ail. Flumiani, who exemplified vanity publishing at its classic worst. Flumiani, the head of Fortuny's and at least two other publishing firms, was accused of having mulcted some five hundred would-be authors of a total of $250,000 in publishing fees by holding out the lure of lush financial returns from sales of books and promising big promotion campaigns and expert editing. The promotion turned out to be a line in a catalog, and the editing was done by a high school girl who "accepted" all legible manuscripts, up to twenty-five of them a day. He also ran a literary agency which, for a small fee, would "place" a manuscript with one of his own firms; a lecture bureau which registered authors at $30 a head (no lectures were ever booked); and something called the Associated Publishers of North America, which attested to the reputability of all his other firms on an impressive letterhead. During his last eighteen months in business, Flumiani issued 117 books and paid out $75 in royalties. A few days after Pearl Harbor, he was sentenced to eighteen months in prison, but he had provided a point of departure for a special kind of publishing enterprise which could not be fully exploited until the war ended.

The article goes on to state that Flumiani was not tried for vanity publishing, which was not and is still not a crime, but for illegally conducting a vanity publishing business.

But he and others like him set the stage and proved that it was a lucrative business. For perspective, that $250,000 he fleeced authors for would be the equivalent of about 4.6 million dollars today.

Outfits like his are able to prosper because of aggressive and expensive marketing campaigns to get in front of authors.

These vampiric-like entities prosper and continue to flourish because they prey so brilliantly on the hopes and dreams of writers. They appear to answer the universal desire to "be published" or to "have a publisher." They also offer mostly useless "smoke and mirror" promotional packages that provide the other thing that seems most elusive to the majority of writers – marketing and publicity.

These predators have always been around in both traditional publishing and self-publishing circles. And over the years, they have continued to adapt their business strategies to evolve as the industry itself has evolved.

Their business model appears to be all kinds of things – and their marketing efforts are powerful and convincing, even to the most skeptic and savvy authors – but it's mostly made up of one sharp focus.

They take money from authors.

No, let me rephrase that.

They take more and more money from authors by making over exaggerated and false promises.

Their business model is typically one where 80% of their revenue comes directly from selling services to authors. They might earn as much as 20% from the sales of books. But that's usually because of the hard work of their authors spending even more money on marketing, often even outside the already mostly useless marketing packages they sell.

Let's take a step back and look at how such businesses can operate and why tens of thousands of them are out there. And also why, like cockroaches, they'll likely always be here regardless of how the industry continues to evolve.

As a writer, you've probably encountered that common response from non-writers that they have always wanted to write a book. Or they have an idea for a book or something along those lines.

Most people have that innate desire to write a book.

Most people, of course, never will.

Why? Because it's damn hard. It takes a lot of determination, hard work, and hours.

But one of the things the Predators rely on is that most people love the idea of writing and publishing a book. That's a huge demographic, particularly since most of those people will never bother to give it a try unless there's an easy shortcut to becoming a published author.

And that's what much of their marketing material plays upon. How easy it is. They do all the work. In some cases, they even just interview the person and hire a ghost writer to craft the book. Simply insert five to ten thousand or more dollars here, and you, too, can be an author. Easy-peasy.

There is a significant amount of money to be made right there. And an endless supply of clientele that will never dry up.

But when it comes to actual authors, those who have done the work and written a book, they come along with the two main promises that are most alluring and difficult to look away from:

- Being published by a publisher
- Marketing and promotions

Let's make sure we understand what a real and proper publisher does.

Broadly, publishing is the act of making information, music, literature, software, and other content available for free or for sale. You are a publisher of content via blogs, YouTube videos, even the various social media platforms like Twitter, Facebook, Instagram, TikTok, and others.)

For the sake of this discussion (and borrowing from the Canadian Oxford dictionary), a publisher is a company that produces and distributes copies of books, newspapers, magazines, etcetera for sale.

A traditional publisher selects the works to be published based upon the raw manuscript's merit, assumes the risk of all the production and publication costs, edits and lays out the author's text, provides the ISBN as well as registration of the book's copyright or national library listing, as well as marketing and distribution. They will typically pay the author an up-front fee, called an advance, for the right to publish the author's work. Ongoing payments (royalties) are paid on a pre-determined schedule based on the sales of the work.

There is something truly compelling about saying that you have a publisher. It comes with some prestige and feelings of worth and importance. Just saying "my publisher" in a sentence appears to come with an air of nobility.

American author James D. MacDonald coined a phrase known in certain literary circles as Yog's Law: "Money should flow toward the author."

This is a rule that I think applies so well when it comes to these predators.

Money should flow to the author.

If the money flows from the author to the "publisher," then you're not dealing with a real publisher. You're dealing with a predator.

And these predators are brilliantly creative and deceptive. They are good at masquerading as publishers but need to be seen for the wolves in sheep's clothing that they are.

One of the most recent name changes I've seen these scam artists use is "hybrid publisher." But over the years, they've used other descriptive phrases like "subsidy publisher," "co-operative publisher," or "collaborative publishing."

Once you are familiar with the signs, it's easy to detect predatory publishing companies. Here are a few things to look out for:

- **Posing as a traditional publisher.** Some vanity publishing outfits will actual call themselves a "real publisher" or refer to themselves as a "traditional publisher." No real publisher ever has to call themselves that or will even refer to vanity publishing because no real publisher ever worries about being seen as a predator. If anywhere on their website they state they aren't a vanity publisher or are a "real publisher," run as fast as you can away from them. I usually adapt Hamlet's "The lady doth protest too much, methinks" perspective and that something more is happening here. Be leery.

- **Promises up front.** Often, on a legitimate publisher's website, there are details about what types of manuscripts they accept, the range of time they are open for submissions, their preferred format, and sometimes expected response rates. Vanity publishers have few of these requirements, but they are filled with promises of the sales, prestige, and money from publishing with them.

- **Terms such as "co-op" or "partnership" or "hybrid" or "shared costs" or "joint venture."** Use of these terms is typically evidence that the vanity publisher will require money from an author. Remember, their profit comes not from selling books but selling services to authors in order to publish.

- **They reach out to you.** A legitimate publisher will rarely email or call you to offer you a publisher contract out of the blue. Yes, it can happen, and it does play into our dreams, desires, and somewhat narcissistic belief that we are that "one in a million" author that publishers will be fighting over. But, like those sleazy and pushy companies looking to offer furnace or air-duct cleaning by showing up at your door or calling you out of the blue, there's more in it for them than for you in cold-calling authors.

- **References/Referrals from Agents/Editors.** If an editor, publisher, or agent you submit a manuscript to replies with any sort of "this is excellent, but it just needs some editing work" and then refers you to a service or sister company, or partner or referred partner, or whatever with a fee for that service, you are most likely dealing with a predator. They are probably either in partnership with or receiving a kickback from the vanity publisher.

- **Avoidance.** Any time you have a reasonable question for one of these vanity publishers and they avoid the question or refuse to give you a clear and concrete answer, they're likely trying to hide something.
- **Distribution and Print on Demand**. The majority of legitimate publishers tend to have relationships with warehouses and bookstores. They most often print and warehouse books available through wholesale distributors and are easily available for bookstores to order and return. While some legitimate publishers use print on demand (POD) technology, they often have bookstore-favorable terms and existing relationships for books to be easily accessible by and available in bookstores (meaning on bookstore shelves and not just an online listing). One way to determine if a publisher is a predator is that they mention where their books will be available. Real publishers don't have to state this. You can also call your local bookstore to see if they have any books from a particular publisher or are able to order any in.
- **Ordering**. Whenever a publisher has details clearly stated on their website requiring order author copies, it might be evidence that their business model isn't to sell books to readers via bookstores but by selling books to authors directly.
- **Pressure**. A real publisher won't pressure an author into signing a contract. They likely also won't phone

an author. They have thousands of other manuscripts sitting in their slush pile. So, any time a "publisher" requires that you reply immediately because this is an offer available only for a limited time, they are playing upon your fears and desire to be accepted and are more than likely counting on that pressure to override your cautious natural logic.

A resource that I recommend every writer bookmark that can help authors determine if a potential publisher is a predatory company is *Writer Beware,* co-founded by Victoria Strauss and available as a resource via SFWA (Science Fiction Writers of America).

The website and resources are easily searchable online, but over at markleslie.ca/publishingpitfalls, you'll find a handy link.

One last thing to keep in mind is that legitimate and honest operating vanity publishers exist. They are typically the ones who state their fees and the services upfront. In addition, they clearly outline what they will do and offer to help prepare, publish and distribute a book prior to an author having even to contact them. These companies are not predators; they are merely service providers operating with transparency and integrity.

PRICING

This pitfall is aimed chiefly at those who self-publish. Pricing can have a dramatic impact on your earnings as an author.

One mistake that authors often make (and this was also covered in **PENNIES**) is setting a single price in their local currency, typically USD, and then not attending to the price in the other main currencies for English language book sales, such as AUD, CAD, EUR, GBP, and NZD.

Neglecting to set "normalized" prices in the other currencies can have a negative impact on the way your book looks to customers on retail websites in those other countries, as well as how they look to the book merchandisers at those retailers who decide what books to feature in different placements on their main web pages.

And you don't want to give potential customers any reason or excuse not to click on that *buy* button. A price that looks "off" can be a subtle yet important factor in providing a subconscious element in the potential reader's mind that throws them off. Sometimes, that's all it takes for them to keep browsing and not buy your book.

Neglecting clean or rounded pricing in those other main currencies can also mean that you're leaving money on the table and not earning the maximum margin for your books.

If you, for example, set a price of 4.99 USD and let the systems take care of the price to auto-convert to other currencies, you'll end up with something like 6.80 AUD and 6.34 CAD.

Customers who see a price like either 6.34 or 6.80 are already subconsciously rounding that price up to 7 in their minds. Rounding to 6.99 AUD and CAD is likely not to lose you any sales, but it will earn you extra margin. It might seem like a bit of "extra change," but let's pretend you sell one hundred copies of your book in both Australia and Canada in a year.

For your Canadian sales, that would come out to an additional $0.65 per unit sale, which is $65. And in Australia, that's $0.19, which works out to $19. That's a total of $84 for a single book. If you have other books, that's extra money that could be in your pocket. Maybe you have five other books. That can be over $400 in extra margin coming your way without actually doing anything. I don't know about you, but I could always put that extra income to good use.

Too often, I see indie authors setting their book prices far too low to begin with. They believe that they are a new author that nobody knows; therefore, no one is likely to take a chance on them. So, they price their full-length novels of 80,000 words, for example, at 2.99 USD.

Yes, I get it. A lower price might be more attractive to some consumers, but it might also indicate lesser quality to some consumers. Think about when you buy products and see something priced abnormally lower or abnormally higher than most of the other products on the market.

Imagine you need to buy laundry detergent. Most of the detergent on the shelf hovers around $12 a bottle. One bottle only costs a dollar. That's a ridiculous price for a bottle of detergent, and you might wonder if there is any soap inside the bottle. At the other end of the shelf, another bottle costs $60. You'd question what could possibly be inside the bottle and how it is worth that much money. You just want to wash your shirt, not go broke. You'd head back to the $12 bottles and make your decision from those reasonable options.

What is the subconscious relation to quality that you may be perceiving with that price differential?

Readers can pass the same type of judgment. You might be losing quality readers who see a price that's too low and pass on it, thinking it must not be that good.

When I worked at Kobo from 2011 to 2017, the company publicly shared that the average price of books sold (and this is across all genres and global currencies) was between $6 and $7. This, of course, accounts for a huge volume of $0.99 and $2.99 indie authored titles and a similar volume of books priced between $10 and $15 or higher from traditional publishers.

In my experience working with thousands of indie authors over the years, it has rarely been their experience that experimentally walking up the price point by $1 increments results in lost revenues. Even if, at certain levels, it might mean a slight decrease in unit sales, the resulting increased margin may more than make up for the difference.

Of course, your readers, your books, your book categories will be unique for different markets, retailers and territories. It's best to experiment, carefully and strategically, by looking at the comparable titles in your categories in those countries to find the right price that earns the best ratio of unit sales and margin.

When experimenting like this, it's vital to consider price as a verb rather than a noun. It doesn't need to be a fixed number forever. What worked once for your book or books might not work the same way as the fluctuations in the marketplace shift. Experiment with your pricing. Adjust up and down and measure the results. That's one of the major benefits of being an indie author. You're in control. Take advantage of that.

Many successful indie authors will also experiment with free in numerous ways. For example, they might make their first book in a series free, offer a free book to get readers to sign up for their mailing list, or give away free copies to reviewers and advance reader teams in exchange for an honest review or "street team" style marketing support.

Making the first book free in your series (when there are at least three or four books in that series) is a great price experiment. It can create a larger funnel of new readers into your books. Those who you've hooked into the world/characters you've created will gladly follow along for the ride, and the benefits of the sales of the remainder of that series can outweigh the "lost revenue" from sales of book one.

This can also work even if you don't write in a series. Making one of your stand-alone books free can also be enough to entice new readers to check out your writing. If they like what you're writing, they may go on to purchase your other books or sign up for your author newsletter, where you're able to continue to communicate with them and potentially sell books to them in the long run.

PRIDE

Pride can negatively impact an author in two different ways.

The first, which is one of the biggest mistakes many authors make, is thinking that their book is for everyone.

Authors spend endless hours and dollars trying to market their book to everyone because they assume it's so universal that anyone would like it.

While we'd all like to believe that to be true about our writing, it takes swallowing a bit of pride to realize that not everything written is going to appeal to every single reader.

And the sooner we accept that there's more of a niche to our readers, the better. Then, we'll stop wasting time, energy, and money trying to put the book in front of everyone and more on putting it in front of the ideal readers or ideal audience.

Related to this are authors who think that their book is so unique that it completely defies all classification. These authors get stuck in saying that it's "not quite this particular genre, but not quite that other genre." Or that it's a cross-genre novel that includes elements from four or five different ones.

Here's the thing: If it can't be classified, it won't be looked at. And you'll be missing out on any of the right people to find it.

It's human nature to classify things. Our very survival as a species evolved from rudimentary classifications of things that were safe and things that were dangerous. That evolution turned to things that are disagreeable, uncomfortable, or painful, compared to things that are stimulating, satisfying, and pleasurable.

People will seek out things they are familiar with that they enjoy. Your book is no different. Sure, it's unique and like nothing other out there. After all, you are the best person to write that specific book.

But your masterful and unique book needs to be understood and appreciated within the context of other books out there in order to find the right readers, those members of your ideal audience, to enjoy it.

Which is why it's important to simplify your unique work down into existing genres, and compare it to similar popular titles, even if those similarities are slight or only partially true.

For example, the movie *Speed* with Sandra Bullock and Keanu Reeves was touted as "*Die-Hard on a bus that can't slow down.*" *Sharknado* was "*Jaws meets Tornado.*" These over-simplifications allow people to consider something already familiar and understand how this new thing might be somewhat like one or more things they already know they have enjoyed.

It does you a huge disservice and prevents you from effective marketing if you aren't able to consider some "comp" (comparable) titles to your unique new work.

Another way that pride can work against an author is when they can't ask for help when they need it. It might come from being afraid to look stupid by asking other writers questions or in an online forum (and thus not getting important information) or failing to recognize the need for getting help in terms of writing, such as a professional editor or cover designer.

But not being willing to ask for help can mean not progressing and improving as a writer.

We get better by working with other professionals, learning, and constantly growing our craft. We grow and expand our abilities and skills when we recognize the need for that continued evolution. And, naturally, along the way, we'll have to reach out; we'll have to ask.

Try to think about asking not as you admitting to not knowing something, but your recognition of the other person's insight and knowledge. You'll be boosting them up just by asking. It could even make their day that you considered them knowledgeable enough to ask.

PRIORITIES

One of my favorite quotes about writing comes from Hugh Prather: "If the desire to write is not accompanied by actual writing, then the desire is not to write."

As a writer, what **are** your priorities?

We will make the time for the things that are most important to us. And we will put off less important things.

That's not fair, you might be saying. *I have so much to do, so many other commitments. I haven't been able to write.*

I'm going to argue that if writing were a priority, you'd find a way to make it happen, even if only in small chunks or segments of each day. Yes, there are commitments and tasks or chores that you can't avoid – sleeping, spending time with, or caring for loved ones, and working, if you have a part-time or full-time job.

But how much time are you spending in front of the television or binge-watching a series on some online streaming service? How about scrolling through a social media feed for that endorphin rush of seeing what you might be missing out on? If you are doing these tasks instead of writing, then you prioritize those things over your writing.

I won't judge you for it. But your priorities are clear. They don't involve writing.

But what if you are overwhelmed with more tasks and commitments than there is time in the day? Or what if you have found yourself in a position where you have more things on your "to do" list than you can feasibly accomplish within a limited chunk of time?

One way of dealing with such things is listing what you need to get done and when each task is due. Next, ask yourself if that deadline is fixed, or is it an artificial one? What is the estimated time or work involved for each? How, when, and where can you get those things done? Is there an external resource or person required that you depend upon to complete any of these items? Have you identified, requested, or informed appropriate third parties of what you're waiting on as well as when you require it? Is there a task someone else is waiting on? Is there a way to communicate with them to determine the impact if you're unable to meet that deadline?

Often, listing out those seemingly overwhelming items and then identifying potential plans or solutions to dealing with them can help you prioritize what you can accomplish on your own, what you need help with, and when you might conceivably get things done.

But breaking them down into individual tasks, smaller items with moderate steps might allow you to make progress and check those small items off the list. In the same way small things can pile-up, they can also have a large impact on removing those items from a previously overwhelming list of things to do.

PRODUCTIVITY

There's no one right way to do things. You'll likely find that your ability to produce depends on a number of factors unique to you. Those factors might change depending on the project you are working on.

Some writers get hung up on the fact that they are not productive in the way that they hear other writers are. Or they believe that they should change the way they are doing something because a successful author in their genre says that's the only way to get things done.

It's easy to get distracted with different techniques, styles, or manners of being productive. Unfortunately, each time you do that can reduce your actual productivity because you spend more time re-learning a method that another author swears by.

Yes, experimentation and trying new things are good. Because the only way to understand what truly works for you is to try it.

But if you are productive, no matter how different or unique your method is for getting the work done, if it's working for you, then stick with it.

If, however, it's **not** working for you, then it's time to attend to or learn a different method or process in order to get the work done that you need to do.

PROGRESSION

Progression goes hand-in-hand with **PRACTICE**. Too often, writers don't recognize the importance of progressing in both the craft and business of writing and publishing.

I explore this in a bit more detail in the book *The 7 Ps of Publishing Success*, but here is how it works, in a nutshell:

Doing the same thing over and over without improving upon it or continuous learning isn't leading to any progression. Are you constantly learning new things, either from the editors you work with or from other writers?

One trait that the people at the top of their industries have in common is their commitment to constantly progressing, learning, and developing their skills and abilities.

For example, Neil Peart, the drummer for the Canadian rock band Rush, recognized across the industry as one of the best drummers of all time, continued to learn from drum mentors, continued to grow and experiment with techniques to improve upon his existing talent. Even with thirty years of experience and numerous accolades, Peart hired a seasoned mentor and re-learned drumming from the very beginning in a completely new way.

International bestselling authors Brandon Sanderson, Mary Robinette Kowal, Howard Tayler, and Dan Wells are some of the hosts of a weekly podcast entitled *Writing Excuses*. They use the tagline: "Fifteen minutes long because you're in a hurry and we're not that smart."

This podcast captures these professional writers who have sold millions upon millions of copies of their books over the decades as they continue to work at and refine their understanding of both the craft and the business of writing.

If internationally respected and award-winning artists like Peart, Sanderson, Kowal, Taylor, and Wells can engage in constantly learning and progressing, so, too, should you and I.

PROFESSIONALISM

While this is one of the elements I talk about in *The 7 Ps of Publishing Success*, I feel it's important to discuss it in *Pitfalls*. That's because an author's professional (or unprofessional) behavior can directly impact their long-term writing success.

Failing to operate and behave professionally in three specific areas can severely limit you and negatively impact your advancement as an author.

- Paperwork, Contracts, and Content
- Interacting and Engaging with Others
- Dealing with Adversity and Rejection

Paperwork, Contracts, and Content

Whether it's the way that you track and manage your stories, books, publishing history, understanding what is published on which platform (indie publishing), and what rights are licensed to which publisher (traditional publishing), or ensuring that the work you produce meets professional standards, this is an easy pitfall for authors to miss.

Simply put, the more organized and structured you are, the more time, energy, hassle, and stress you will save in the long run.

If you make a commitment, regardless of whether it is a contract with a publisher, an agreement with another author, or someone else within the industry, you keep that commitment. And if you are not ensuring the content you send to publishers or release to the market directly doesn't meet basic minimal quality requirements, you are demonstrating to industry people and readers that you are not a professional.

Interacting and Engaging with Others

Whether you like it or not, people are paying attention to the way that you treat others. Similarly, the way you appear, either in person or on your website or social media, can have an extremely negative impact on the way people perceive you. On the plus side, it can have a significant positive effect if you handle it with care.

If you show up to in-person events looking like a slob, people will most likely think you are disorganized, sloppy, and don't care about your appearance. I'm not saying you have to wear fancy or fashionable clothes. Your appearance might necessarily be related to your overall author branding, which can be one of many different styles.

I hate having to say this, but I've seen it enough times that I must: shower or bathe, brush your teeth, fix your hair. If you look like you just rolled out of bed, people will assume you take the same care in your writing. And if you or your breath smell, you'll be avoided and remembered in that negative way.

Similarly, if you treat people with a similar disregard, others notice. It not only reflects poorly on you, but your behavior and attitude are not something people will soon forget. You might be wearing the result of a moment where you treated someone else with disrespect for years, which could lead to lost opportunities. Nobody wants to work with a jerk. So do your best not to be a dick or to treat others poorly.

Dealing with Adversity and Rejection

Whether you are traditional publishing or indie publishing, rejection and adversity are two common companions. From rejections of your manuscript to one-star reviews (or perhaps even worse, no reviews at all, that frustrating sound of crickets to your latest release), the road is not always paved with gold. If anything, the road is often carved up with jagged pieces of asphalt, rocks, and the occasional bit of broken glass seeking to deflate your tires.

How you deal with these things can impact your ability to stick it out for the long run and your image as a professional.

Have bad things come your way? There might be a handful of trusted colleagues or loved ones you can share your angst and grief with. But public (or online) social displays can make you come off like a pouty sad sack, or perhaps Doug or Wendy Whiner from classic *Saturday Night Live* sketches.

Yes, it's important to blow off steam or share negative things, particularly if it's helpful to others in the industry to be aware of something, such as warning other writers about a bad experience with a company, product, or person.

But before you publicly clench your fists and stomp and storm, consider how it might appear to others who may end up perceiving you as a big sucky baby who just can't handle the realities of living in a grown-up's world.

And never, *ever* comment on or respond to a bad review. That's about as useful as going online and trying to have an intelligent debate about deeply rooted political differences. It's not like you're going to change the other person's mind. It'll only inflate the hostility and adversity of the situation. Even a well-intended and polite response to a negative review is likely going to be misinterpreted and misunderstood. It's best to avoid it. Brush yourself off, pick yourself up, and move on.

The writing and publishing business is hard. There's a lot of work involved and a significant amount of adversity. Readers and others within the industry are paying attention to how you react when the going gets tough.

If you'd like to see an example of how deep an impression unprofessional behavior can leave, I have ranted about unprofessional author behavior on my podcast. Most recently, in Episode 203 – A Rant on Unprofessional Behavior (July 2021), I explain the impact of writers who commit to something that requires others to do a lot of work and then back out without a single warning or word.

Don't be that author.

PROMOTION

One universal commonality among writers is related to promotion and marketing. While some writers enjoy marketing and promotional activities, many will claim it's the thing they dread and avoid the most.

There are many misperceptions about marketing and promotions that authors immediately adopt, which make things harder than they need to be.

The first is that just having a publisher doesn't mean you'll automatically have someone else taking care of your marketing and promotions. I explain in a bit more detail in **Publishers**. But just know that it doesn't matter which publishing path you take; you won't be able to avoid having to promote your writing in one way or another.

The second is that authors often make promotions and marketing into something harder than it has to be by convincing themselves they don't know how to do it or that it's too hard. The reality, as Diana Wink of *Story Artist Podcast* brilliantly explained to me in Episode 187 of the *Stark Reflections on Writing and Publishing Podcast* (Business Minded Creative Marketing with Diana Wink), was that marketing is just a type of storytelling. The consumer has something they want or need, and the marketing is sharing a story that helps them find a solution they'll enjoy.

Taking that perspective, writers seem to be perfectly inclined to be doing promotions and marketing since they are already storytellers.

In addition to that, nobody knows your writing, your books, your stories, quite like you do. And nobody else is likely ever going to be as passionate about your writing as you are.

This isn't to say that you won't need help along the way or have to leverage paid resources or even hire people. But you do have to take ownership over promotional activity. You do need to accept that it's a part of the writing and publishing life.

Here are some of the pitfalls within the realm of promotion to be cautious of along the way.

Promoting Too Early

One of the biggest pitfalls related to promotions that authors fall prey to is spending a lot of time, energy, and money promoting their first book.

Many promotional activities cost a minimal amount of money. Earning your investment back on the margin of the sale of a single book might not work as well as if there aren't additional books (whether they are in a series or not) that readers who have found you due to this investment can go on to purchase and read.

Promoting To the Wrong Audience

If you haven't taken the time to fully understand who your work is for, as specifically as possible, you might be spending time and money pushing your work in front of the wrong readers.

Social Media

Writers will often jump on a social media platform in response to a popular trend because they hear that some author used that platform to sell a ton of their work.

TikTok is a recent example. There were numerous stories out in mid-2021 about how some authors had sold an outrageous number of books because of some activity on that platform.

Thousands of authors rushed to TikTok, thinking it would be the magic bullet that would suddenly grow their audience and sell thousands of copies of their books. The reality is that social media is nothing more than a digital place that people "gather" and share content. It takes work, effort, and engaging in a community to find success, or more often than not, accidentally fall back into some lucky random lightning strike algorithm that makes one's content go viral.

Test and check out social media platforms, but if you're not enjoying the engagement and the work involved in creating content for that platform, you might not want to waste your time.

Like writing itself, it's a lot of work. Why fall down that rabbit hole and lose time from other things that might benefit your long-term writing career?

Publicist

Outsourcing promotions might work well but be careful of who and how you hire. What they actually offer and can do for you can vary dramatically, leading to huge disappointment and lost money. See **PUBLICISTS** for more details.

Testing, Experimentation, and Analysis

Too often, writers fall into the trap of running a promotion or advertising campaign because they heard it was the thing to do, that everyone else was doing it.

So they set up an ad on Facebook, Amazon Advertising, BookBub, or wherever, and just let it ride, without first testing it out, measuring results, before diving in with a larger budget.

This can result in the slow (or fast) bleed of money and promotional funds.

Each platform works differently. Measures and results will differ based on what you are advertising, where you are advertising, and as time passes.

There are plenty of fantastic resources, both paid and free, helping authors learn how to leverage different platforms. Finding success on those platforms usually involves a combination of listening to other authors who have figured out some of the strategies that work, testing and trying out small promotions, measuring the effect, then adjusting, measuring and analyzing again, then tweaking.

It's not easy, and it takes a significant amount of time and energy. And you may find, after experimenting, that some platform just doesn't work for your particular book or genre, or whatever it is you're trying to generate results for. That's okay. Move on and try another one.

Paid Newsletters

There are hundreds of paid newsletters out there. These are platforms where readers sign up to be notified of books that are either free or discounted in specific genres via the various eBook reading platforms. Authors and publishers then apply for their books to be considered to be included in the email blast to those readers on a particular day, agreeing to reduce or remove the price of their eBook for a specified time frame.

Like traditional publishing, it's often a highly curated selection. The newsletter platform might have only one hundred submissions for only two spots. But this careful curation is what makes these newsletters successful. There might be several hundred thousand subscribers to that newsletter, meaning your book will get in front of the eyes of a significant number of the right readers, helping to boost sales of your book.

As of the writing of this book, BookBub Feature Deals arc among the most expensive, but also the most lucrative, of the newsletters. But there are hundreds of them out there.

Like any other promotional activity, it will likely take some experimentation to find the newsletters that work best for you and your books. There will also be some duds or platforms that make grandiose promises and provide little value in return.

Other authors are a great resource for determining which newsletters tend to work best but make sure you attune to the similarities and differences of your books to their books. You can find listings of recommended paid newsletters on numerous sites, such as the Alliance of Independent Authors, Reedsy, and the *Wide for the Win* Facebook group.

Push Push Push

It's important to promote and market both your author brand and your books, but there is a fine balance that's important to establish. Otherwise, you might be seen as that annoying author who is constantly doing nothing but pushing their book or books onto others.

I get into this in more detail under **PUSHY**, but I wanted to mention it here because it often falls under promotional activities.

PROOFREADING

Authors often mistake the term editing for "proofreading" which ultimate refers to checking for spelling mistakes, punctuation errors, typos, word choice confusion, and formatting issues.

Proofreading is critically important, but it is **not** editing. If you hire a proofreader, they are not the same as an editor. Proofreading is a light, last-step form of editing, but it's not the same as the type of work that a developmental editor or a copy editor does.

Sometimes it can be useful to have a work proofread before sending it to an editor. If an editor who does more developmental or structural or copyediting work has to deal with typos and other minor mistakes, it can mean they have to spend more time on your manuscript, thus costing you more time and money.

Prior to submitting a manuscript to an editor, doing a proofread yourself, having a trusted person do one, or leveraging an automated proofreading and grammar tool such as Grammarly or ProWritingAid can save you time and money.

In addition, after you complete an edit and rewrite, and even after the book is laid out for eBook and print, a proofread can be important in catching any new issues introduced to the manuscript.

One of the most reliable proofreading exercises I have found for proofreading myself is reading the manuscript aloud, such as when I am recording the audiobook version of a manuscript.

Another tip for proofreading is printing off the final file. We're often able to recognize issues in print that our eyes might miss when looking at it on a screen. You might also consider reading the manuscript line by line and backward so that you can capture potential typos and grammar errors without getting "caught up" in the story that sometimes results in automatically "correcting" a textual error subconsciously.

PUBLISH

In order to sell books, you actually have to publish something. It might seem like a silly thing to pause and talk about, but it's not. I'm mentioning it because I've seen it time and again. And it's definitely a pitfall that writers can fall prey to.

Whether you want to sell your writing to a traditional publishing market or self-publish it, you can't sell until you have something to sell.

I was tempted to call this segment **PUBLISH OR PER-ISH**. That phrase, which is attributed to a 1932 book by Harold Jefferson Coolidge, is a maxim that summarizes the pressure for faculty and scholars to publish academic work to succeed in academia. It's somewhat applicable here because, regardless of how you define success as an author, it typically involves your work being consumed, in some manner, by readers.

If readership without income, for example, is a goal, there are numerous options for publishing that are free to use and gatekeeper-free. There's no shortage of options, from blogs and other online publications filled with community-driven content to platforms like Wattpad and so many others that allow writers to publish their writing for free and then be consumed by readers for free.

But assuming that you're also interested in earning money as an author, you need to submit your writing to various markets in the hopes that an agent, editor, or publication accepts and publishes your work, or you need to publish it yourself via the numerous options available.

There was an old saying I remember from growing up in the traditional publishing world. "A manuscript doesn't sell in a drawer." Instead, it has to be mailed out to a market looking to acquire that type of work.

Similarly, a brilliantly crafted book you have worked on, paid out funds for editing and a professional cover isn't going to sell if you don't hit that publish button.

I get it. It's scary.

It's not easy putting yourself out there and being judged. Because you will be judged. Not everyone who comes upon and reads your work will like it. And that's something that never gets easier, no matter how long you've been writing and publishing.

This is likely why this can be a major pitfall. Perhaps it's one you have been in or are currently stuck in.

I'm not sure what I can say to help you through that, other than this:

What's the worst thing that can happen if you make your work available to an agent, editor, or the public?

They don't like it? They leave a bad review? Nobody buys or reads it?

Sure, those are all possibilities.

But if you don't publish, you're guaranteed that nobody is going to buy or read it.

PUBLISHERS

From the traditional and literary perspective, real publishers are persons or companies that produce and distribute copies of books, newspapers, magazines, etcetera for sale. They are responsible for curating and selecting the works to be published; they assume the risk of production and publication costs. They edit and publish an author's work and provide distribution and marketing of that work. They normally pay an advance to the author and ongoing royalties based upon sales of that work.

In any case where the money does not flow to the author, you aren't dealing with what I call a real publisher. You're dealing with a vanity press; a subsidy publishing company trying to masquerade as a publisher. They engage in nefarious and deceptive practices in order to trick authors into believing they are signing their rights to a legitimate publisher. Please read more about them under **PREDATORS**.

When it comes to actual publishers, just because a publisher is assuming all the risk of the costs of publishing, producing, and distributing a book doesn't mean that there aren't pitfalls to avoid when working with them.

Below are a few of the publisher pitfalls to be aware of and cautious of.

Contracts

It's critical that you remember that a contract is a negotiation that is not set in stone until both parties agree upon the details and sign them.

Publisher contracts are typically cookie-cutter templates filled with a number of boilerplate rights requests.

Some of the clauses put into a publishing contract are by default and can easily be struck or modified. All you need to do is ask.

And yes, you can and should ask for anything that you are not comfortable signing. I learned this after reading Kristine Kathryn Rusch's 2013 book **Dealbreakers: *Contract Terms Writers Should Avoid***. (She since revised the content from that book into the 2016 book **Closing the Deal on Your Terms: *Agents, Contracts and Other Considerations*.**) Reading that 2013 book provided me with enough knowledge to ask for twelve changes to a publishing contract I had signed that year. The publisher accepted ten of the twelve requests. The last two weren't dealbreakers, just "nice-to-have" items. And so, I was set.

Some of the clauses you should look out for are:

- **Formats** – Publisher contracts are, by default, going to want the publisher to have all rights regardless of whether or not they actually exploit them. They might, for example, desire audiobook rights without ever producing a single audiobook. (This can go for other formats as well). If they request a format you know they don't produce, you can suggest or require striking it from the contract, so you're free to offer it to another publisher or publish that format yourself.

- **Language** – Similar to the above mention, publishers might request rights to all languages, regardless of whether or not they ever publish in that language. If they don't publish in the other language or languages and aren't specifically offering you money for those rights, there's no need for them to lock up those rights. Remove this clause and free yourself up to sell foreign language rights directly to another publisher.

- **Option** – The right of the publisher to acquire the publishing rights to the next book by the author. This usually comes with the author agreeing not to send the work to another publisher or publish it by other means. Be careful of this. Depending on the language used in this clause, it could be the publisher locking you into the next book, removing your possibility of a larger advance from a competing publisher, or publishing it yourself.

- **Right of First Refusal** – Similar to the option right mentioned above, publishing contracts often have a "right of first refusal" clause, which requires that they be offered the next book or books that they can decide to publish or reject before the author sends it to another publisher or publishes by another means. This option is slightly more open than the aforementioned one. In addition, while you're obligated to show the next book manuscript to that publisher, you usually aren't required to accept their terms and can, after you show them and if they make an offer, reject their terms.

- **Rights Reversion** – When you sign a contract with a publisher, it typically allows them the rights to publish your book. But when and how do those rights return to you, the author. Is it a fixed date? Is it dependent upon a measurable factor such as sales quantity in a specified time? How can an author initiate the reversion of rights? These are all things to pay attention to.

Confirmation Bias

There are two ways that confirmation bias within a publishing house can be a pitfall for writers.

The first is related to the marketing that a writer puts into your book. With the exception of smaller publishers with limited budgets, the amount of money a publisher will spend on marketing your book when it is published is typically proportional to the advance you receive.

If you are a beginning or midlist writer who has received a modest advance in your publishing contract, the investment in marketing your book is likely to be similarly modest.

Internal publicists and marketing departments within publishing houses work to ensure that the publisher earns back the investment made for each book they publish.

For example, if your advance/offer is $1,000, but that same publisher offered another author $100,000, guess which book is more likely to receive the majority of time, attention, and care from the PR, marketing, and sales teams from that publisher? Which book/author are they more likely to spend most of their time and energy on? Typically, the author with a larger advance likely already had a huge fan following, and likely doesn't need the same time, care, and attention that a lesser known, newer author could use.

If, for example, both Stephen King and I are with the same publisher (although, let's be clear here, King's advance would be significantly higher), the publicity and marketing from the publisher for his book would be one thousand or more times any publicity offered for my book. And yet, given the author's stature, his book would likely sell a million plus copies on release day without any push or marketing campaign needed. All people would need to know is that King has a new book, which rabid fans would already know. Bookstores would, of course, already be ensuring plenty of stock for one of the world's bestselling authors.

The second way confirmation bias can affect an author is in the acquisition process itself and how they react to author submissions.

Publishers, editors, and agents are among the brightest, most passionate people in the book industry. Many of them come with decades of dedication to publishing.

However, even with all this experience, insight, knowledge, and passion, they still make mistakes.

Regardless of all the curation and analytics and the gambler-like weighing of that gut feeling versus estimations and calculations they make, only about 20% of all the books they publish earn money.

Despite this, they believe that they know, better than anyone, which genres, topics, and styles are hot, and which ones will be blockbuster bestsellers.

They often reject fantastic books because they believe that "nobody is reading that any longer" or "that was hot three years ago, not now."

Remember that publishers aren't publishing books to sell books directly to readers. They are acquiring rights to publish books that they are trying to sell mostly to chain and larger bookstore buyers specifically to fit within a four-season selling cycle of the book industry.

"Nobody is reading that any longer" might actually be their way of saying, "When we pitched a book like this to Barnes & Noble, they didn't order enough copies of it."

For this reason, publishers pass on thousands of excellent titles each year. And yet, those same books are likely to sell enough copies to earn the self-published author more than the advance they likely would have been offered by a publisher. The same is true for the next element listed below.

Conflict of Interest

As more and more smaller publishing houses get absorbed into large conglomerates, publishers have reduced the number of books they publish due to them not wanting to create as many conflicting titles to "split the vote" of the consumer.

For this reason, publishers will often reject outstanding books, not because they don't have any merit, but because they "recently published a book in that category, or with a similar topic" from that or one of their sister imprints.

This means that they regularly reject submissions not based on how good that book is but instead because they aren't able to fit it into a constantly tightening and limiting list of titles they can publish in a specified period.

Again, just because a publisher rejected a manuscript doesn't mean there isn't an audience for it or that it's not worthy of publication.

They might have rejected it because of the potential conflict of interest with another similar title they already have scheduled for release in the coming quarter or year.

Marketing

Authors often state that they want a publisher because they don't want to do their own marketing. The reality is that publishers will typically only market a book for the first month, or perhaps as long as the first three to six months, of a book's release. (It's more often the first month or even the first few weeks of a book's release).

This is because the in-house publicists have limited time to spend on each new release.

While your book is your precious and special baby, the publicist might by working simultaneously on a handful, or even dozens, of other authors and titles released in that same period of time.

Your book is not likely to be the center of their attention and efforts for more than a very limited time. Remember (as mentioned in the **Conflict of Interest** note): the publicist is more likely to be investing in a much more intense fashion in any of the big-name authors or authors who have received a much higher advance for their book.

So, if you're thinking that having a publisher means not having to do any marketing, I'm afraid you are sadly mistaken.

PUBLICISTS

Mentioning that they have a publicist seems to come with some cachet for writers, perhaps in a similar way that they can talk about their agent. It can feel like having a key to the executive washroom when an author responds to a query with: "My publicist will get back to you."

But it's good for authors to know what a publicist does and what a publicist doesn't do. Similarly, it's important to realize the differences in the way publicists can work that may or may not tie in with your expectations and budget.

So tread carefully.

A book publicist's job is to create awareness for you and your book. It is usually through press releases, article pitches, feature stories, mentions, or appearances on television and radio. The publicist is an author's liaison with the media. Their goal is to generate interest and coverage of an author and their works.

Many people believe that having a publisher means you have a publicist. That might be true, depending on your publisher and your status as an author. Even if you do have a publicist, if you're a beginning writer with a minimal audience and a low advance, the publisher's publicist is not going to spend much time working on your book. And yes, it's an unfair self-fulfilling prophecy. They are likely applying more effort to getting a larger name author or title opportunities and appearances.

Since their goal is results with media bookings, appearances, and coverage, they'll have more luck with the bigger name author. So, from their perspective, why try to push a giant boulder up a steep incline when they can push another one down a large slope with far less effort?

In addition, a publisher's publicist is only working on books and authors for a limited amount of time. Most likely, they're only focusing on a new book for the first month or nine to twelve weeks after a book's release. If they are a larger publisher, the publicist has numerous authors and titles to juggle and is, thus, likely only spending a minimal amount of time on your books.

Many believe that self-published authors **need** a publicist since they don't have a publisher to represent them. And, in many ways, a publicist can be one of those freelancers that allows indie authors the opportunity to leverage hired expertise and operate professionally.

Here is what an independent book publicist (i.e., a freelancer who authors can hire) can do for an author:

- **Contacts** – Publicists usually have many contacts and relationships with people in the industry and media.
- **Standing Out** – In the US alone, thousands of books are published every single day. A publicist can give you a competitive edge.
- **Marketing Expertise** – Publicists usually come with experience and understanding of marketing, particularly when it comes to marketing books and authors for promotional content/appearances.

- **Brand Building** – Publicists can focus on one specific book, several books, or a new release. They can also help authors build and maintain a professional brand.
- **Coaching** – Many authors are not comfortable with media appearances (radio, podcast, television). Some publicists can coach authors on preparing for such events to come off their best.
- **Workload Support** – You already have so much to do as an author. Having a publicist focus on reaching out to media and other contacts can save you time to focus on your writing or other aspects of your business.

If you are looking to hire a publicist, be aware that different ones offer various perks. Some are great at one or two of the elements above but might not be as good at others. Therefore, it's critically important to do some homework ahead of time and ensure your publicist is a good fit for you.

Advice when looking for a publicist

- Ensure they understand you, your genre, your niche as an author
- Inquire or look for references and testimonials from authors who have worked with them
- Find out their specific areas of expertise or tasks they can help with. What do they do best? Different publicists have different strengths. Some are great at booking media appearances, others at

booking in-person events, launches, and book signings, others are connected to book reviewers and book bloggers.

- Engage in a conversation with the publicist to see if they are a good fit for you. This is a relationship, so it needs to be one you are both comfortable with.

We've looked at the positives and all the good things a publicist can offer, now let's ground ourselves in a bit of reality. While a publicist can provide valuable services, they can also be a deadly money trap for writers who don't properly understand what they **can** and often **can't** do for a writer.

A publicist can open doors for an author, particularly if they have valuable contacts that align with your author brand and your books. However, if there's no track record of existing clients' appearances in media outlets or other high-profile coverage, be leery.

All a publicist can do is help with visibility, coverage, and brand awareness for you or your books.

They cannot guarantee book sales.

And it is extremely difficult to measure the impact a publicist has on overall book sales. So, if you're an author who only likes to operate in detailed analytics and a precise conversion to sales - Facebook or Amazon Advertising ad cost X dollars and resulted in Y number of views, Z number of clicks, etc. - you'll be disappointed that there are no such measures in this realm.

Be aware that no publicist can **ever** offer you any guarantees. So if you are considering a publicist and you see that they guarantee specific things that seem amazing and perhaps even too-good-to-be-true, they likely are.

If a publicist says they can guarantee you specific media placements, book ranking on major sites and bestseller lists, or a particular increase in sales, it's best to avoid them.

In addition, when looking at hiring a publicist, the question might not be: "*Should* I hire a publicist?" Instead, it might more aptly be: "Can I *afford* a publicist?"

Experienced publicists can charge upwards of $3000 to $5000 per month. And remember, that comes with no guarantees of coverage, reviews, or sales.

Can you afford that?

For me, the answer for years was a resounding: "No!"

But that changed in late 2020 when I hired a publicist. This was after spending a couple of years paying attention to a particular publicist I had met in person at a conference and conducted a live interview with about book publicity. I later interviewed him for my podcast.

It was about midway through my interview in Episode 163 – Getting a Creative Edge with Mickey Mikkelson that I believed there would be a good fit in hiring Mickey as my publicist.

He operates in a "pay for placement" or "pay for performance" (P4P) model, which still seems to be rare among book publicists. Like any model, authors need to be cautious of this method. There are always slick, smooth, and sleazy operators in this industry preying on an author's hopes and dreams.

But in this case, the way Mickey operates and how he charges clients works nicely for me. He has a P4P model with a monthly cap. The monthly cap set in place with my contract with him is dramatically below the outrageous monthly retainer fees mentioned earlier in this chapter and aligns well within a budget I'm comfortable with.

Not every booking has been worth it, and, over time, Mickey has adjusted his approach to align me with the proper contacts and outlets based on my feedback.

But some of them have been truly spectacular and more than make up for the occasional miss. If I were investing that same money in specific types of ads, such as Amazon or Facebook ads, for example, it would also come with a significant amount of labor costs, and I'd likely experience a similar percentage of misses.

At the end of the day, it's a relationship. I trust Mickey to represent me professionally and continue to find opportunities that save me time and allow me to focus more on writing. For me, the combination of affordability and the time saving – not to mention the cachet that comes with being able to post that Creative Edge Publicity represents me – is well worth it.

But you, as an author, need to carefully measure and consider whether a publicist is a worthwhile expense. If you are a newer writer, with perhaps only one book, significant marketing expenses such as a publicist may be harder to earn back.

I published my first book in 2004, and I hired a publicist in 2020, sixteen years later. Of course, you needn't wait that long, but note that one of the reason the math works well for me is I have more than twenty books, meaning the coverage Mickey gets me can lead to sales of more than one of my books, helping me earn that investment back more quickly.

And take care, because if you pick the wrong publicist, you can bleed a significant amount of money with no return on that investment.

PURPOSE

Simon Sinek, co-author of **Find your Why:** *A Practical Guide for Discovering Purpose for You and Your Team,* *and author of Start with Why: How Great Leaders Inspire Everyone to Take Action,* says that when people learn their why, it makes them more confident and more competent to find ways to make choices and a life in which they are more likely to feel fulfilled.

What is your purpose, what is your cause, what do you believe?

Because that drives the how and the what that you do.

Something drives you to want to compose words in ways that compel other people to read them.

But asking the question of what your purpose for writing is might enlighten you in ways that help you continue even when inspiration doesn't strike, even when the challenges of finding success seem overly daunting, and even when no other extrinsic factors are motivating you.

Knowing your why, knowing the reason you write or want to write is a powerful motivating factor to help you continue forward.

Not knowing your purpose can cause you to succumb to all the various pitfalls and challenges that stop many writers in their tracks.

Because, as Nietzsche said in the 1889 **Twilight of the Idols,** "If we have our own 'why' of life, we shall get almost with almost any 'how.'" Or, as Viktor Frankl adapted it in his 1946 **Man's Search for Meaning,** "He who has a why to live for, can bear with almost any how."

PUSHY

Nobody likes a pushy and aggressive salesperson. Nobody wakes up in the morning and thinks: "I'd like someone to sell me something today."

And very few people are enamored with that slick and sleazy guy at a group gathering who forces his way into a conversation, dominates it by talking about himself and what he does for a living, then always brings the conversation back to why his business (let's say he's a life insurance salesman) is something everybody needs. He usually thrusts his business cards into everyone's hands then moves on to conquer the next group.

Unless he's ridiculously charming and entertaining (i.e., bringing some value to that conversation), that guy is usually annoying and disruptive.

Nobody enjoys talking to **that** guy.

And you definitely don't want to be thought of as **that** guy.

Or, in our case, **that** author.

Yes, authors need to be proud of and willing to talk about their books. Yes, authors need to be constantly promoting. But authors also need to walk a very fine line and learn ways to read a room and determine if it's the right time or place.

It's not easy to find that balance, and this is a trap that many authors can fall into under the guise that marketing and promoting their books is an important activity.

Where and how do you find that balance? It's not easy. But let's start with a few basic principles.

First, people tend to do business with or buy things from people they know, like, and trust. Getting to know other people and being involved in a discussion or community beyond your book and your writing is an excellent place to start. You're far more than just an author and far more than just the author of any one work. You're deeper, richer, nuanced, and dynamic. Be that. Be genuine. Be authentic. And listen.

You're far more likely to find that people are interested in you first and then the things you write.

Second, consider your target audience. Not everyone is your target reader; not everyone is going to want to read the things you've written and published. However, they might, particularly if you are interesting, charming, genuine, and an engaging part of a dynamic conversation or interaction, end up being an advocate for you, or your books, to someone they know who is in your ideal demographic.

This holds for both in-person interactions as well as across social media. For example, how do you respond when you look at an author's Twitter, Facebook, or Instagram feed, and all you see are blatant "buy my book" messages? Compare that to how you feel if those same feeds are a nuanced balance of interesting, informative, or amusing posts, anecdotes, shares of, or even promoting other people's content.

I have found that the 80/20 principle works effectively in both social media and personal interactions. Provide content, share, and push others 80% of the time. Then, 20% of the time, talk about or push your own content. The balance skews toward providing and giving rather than asking or taking.

You come across as less of a douche.

Let's consider, for a moment, an example of in-person selling. Imagine you're at a local craft fair or convention or perhaps a bookstore with a table of your books in front of you. People are walking by, and there's a chance to interact with and sell books to them.

One approach is (and yes, this is not easy for many authors who can be introverted most of the time) turning on the "salesman" charm and pushing your book at everyone. The other is being personable and talking with them, and establishing a connection with them. It takes more time and energy.

Yes, I get it that sometimes, when you are pushy and aggressive, people might buy from you. They might buy because of the pressure they were under. They might buy out of guilt. Or even pity. So, you might have made a sale at that moment. But it was a transaction that likely left the person buying from you with a bad taste in their mouth.

Consider the long-term when it comes to your success as an author. Would you rather sell one book today, with the cost of all else unconsidered, or potentially gain a reader for life who is genuinely interested in you and your books?

The person forced into buying a book from you might end up spreading word of mouth about the negative experience, which isn't good for your books or your author brand.

The person genuinely interested in you, even if they aren't your ideal reader, or didn't buy one of your books that day, might go on to talk about you with people they know who would enjoy your books.

Take me and my writing, for example.

When I'm doing an in-person event, I have a life-sized skeleton (Barnaby Bones) with me. Where applicable, I have décor such as skulls and other spooky items which clearly illustrate the type of books I have: true ghost story books, dark thrillers, urban fantasy, and Twilight Zone-style tales.

It's not everybody's cup of tea. But it's certainly eye-catching and draws people in. It is also an amazing conversation starter, particularly since I lean towards reserved and introverted in basic social interactions. I'm much more comfortable if someone starts a conversation with me than me starting a conversation.

Because what I write is not for everyone, I know there's a long shot of selling. But folks love to talk about macabre topics, and ghosts, and such. So, I'm happy to chat with them and listen to them sharing their own scary experiences.

There have been plenty of times when I found out that a person I was speaking with wasn't interested in the types of books I write but was interested in a different genre or style of book. I did my best to make an appropriate recommendation to them. I might suggest a book from a friend who does write in that genre or some other title I legitimately thought they might enjoy.

There's no way to measure if that ever had a positive effect, but at the very least, even if they didn't purchase anything, that person left an interaction with me with some information, or some entertainment, or potentially some value (if I was able to recommend something in line with their tastes).

It might result in then talking about meeting an author (a hopefully memorable author with a skeleton and other creepy stuff at his author table) to one or more friends over the course of the next few days, weeks, months, or even years, who is definitely in to the type of thing I write.

And it could lead to a long-term impression rather than a single interaction with a pushy and aggressive author who wouldn't shut up about their books.

As Del Griffith says in the movie *Planes, Trains and Automobiles*, "The last thing I want to be remembered as is an annoying blabbermouth." While that character, played by actor John Candy in the classic 1987 John Hughes movie, may be annoying, he is also deep and nuanced, and someone Neal Page (Steve Martin's character) comes to care for and admire by the end of the film's 93-minute run.

Unfortunately, you don't often get that sort of chance.

You often only get a single moment, a single chance to make an impression.

What do you want that impression to be?

Hopefully, it's not **that** guy.

CONCLUSION

I hope you found this collection of potential publishing pitfalls poignant.

There might even be particular topics or elements that you're surprised I didn't include.

For example, I had originally intended to include something on **PROCRASTINATION,** but I kept putting it off.

[*Insert pause, waiting for the pun to be detected*]

In all seriousness, procrastination can be a serious issue that prevents authors from getting things done, most significantly writing that manuscript, submitting it to a publisher, or taking the steps to self-publishing. But for me, procrastination is a tool that I leverage. I work to deadline, and I always have. It's just part of the process I have developed as a writer.

I had trouble outlining the negatives associated with procrastination, even though there are many. (Just ask my editor, for example). But that's part of the **PERCEPTION** by which I created this book. Everything is skewed based upon that.

So perhaps there are other elements you thought might appear in this book that didn't come up.

Similarly, I'm assuming there are points or areas that you didn't see as a pitfall because, for you, it's not an issue, or it's something you're already leveraging in a powerful way.

If that's the case, then that is fantastic. Because we are all unique and have our own paths. None of those paths are the same for different writers.

And I would love to hear your thoughts on any of those missing Ps. I just might add them to a future edition of this book. Or, better yet, they just might be the basis for a constructive and informative conversation about writing and publishing.

So, feel free to email me (mark@markleslie.ca) and let me know your thoughts and comments. Also, if you're so inclined, leave an honest review on the retailer of your choice. I'm sure that you, as an author, understand just how critically important those can be.

Finally, thanks for reading. I hope that you can leverage some of what you've just read in a way that helps you avoid at least some of the pitfalls of the writing and publishing life. No, we can't avoid them all, but hopefully, we are educated and informed about those that may lie on that path ahead.

Yours in writing,
Mark Leslie Lefebvre
August 2021

RESOURCES

Further resources and references to various books, articles, podcasts, and other sources applicable for further learning can be found on my website at:

www.markleslie.ca/publishingpitfalls

ABOUT THE AUTHOR

Mark's highly successful experience in the publishing and bookselling industry spans more than three decades. He has worked in almost every type of brick and mortar, online and digital bookstore.

The former Director of self-publishing and author relations for Rakuten Kobo, and the founding leader of *Kobo Writing Life*, Kobo's free direct-to-Kobo publishing tool, Mark thrives on innovation, particularly as it relates to digital publishing.

He writes full-time and mentors and coaches authors and publishers about digital publishing opportunities both 1:1 and via his Stark Reflections on Writing & Publishing weekly podcast.

You can learn more about Mark at www.markleslie.ca

Selected Books by the Author

Under the name Mark Leslie Lefebvre

Stark Publishing Solutions

The 7 Ps of Publishing Success

Killing It on Kobo

An Author's Guide to Working with Libraries and Bookstores

Wide for the Win

Co-authored titles

Taking the Short Tack: *Creating Income and Connecting with Readers using Short Fiction*

(with Matty Dalrymple)

The Relaxed Author: *Take the Pressure off Your Art and Enjoy the Creative Journey*

(with Joanna Penn)